MY NAME IS
VICTORIOUS
TEEN EDITION

Find Strength, Freedom, and Joy
in Who You Are Created to Be

Lori Wilhite
Emma Wilhite

My Name Is Victorious - Teen Edition: Find Strength, Freedom, and Joy in Who You Are Created to Be

Copyright © 2018 Lori Wilhite

ISBN 978-0-578-20777-3

Editing by Eric Stanford
Book design by Brian Hurst

Printed and bound in USA
First printing September 2018

Published by Leading and Loving It
1001 New Beginnings Dr
Henderson, Nevada, USA 89011

Visit mynameisvictorious.com

first name

Danielle

middle name

Dolores

last name

D'Andrea

preferred name

Danielle

nicknames

Table of Contents

Session 3

Session 4

I've been called many names. My dad calls me Beautiful. My mom calls me Sissy. My friends call me Emootie (long story). And my Algebra teacher called me Emmy White. Uh. Not my name, Mr Zirpoli. Not my name.

We all have names we carry around with us. Some of them are wonderful, and we wear them with pride. Others, not so much.

My brother was recently asked which animals best describe each of our family members and why. He declared that me, his sweet sister, was a cat—a really annoying cat. His dieting dad was pronounced a hippo—a hungry, hungry hippo. And his loving mom was *drumroll, please* a sloth. A sloth?! Score one for Ethan.

Of course, my mom immediately told him to choose animals that reflect the positive qualities of our family. You'll get 'em next time, dude.

I was then transformed into a cheetah, since I am a much faster runner than him.

Dad became a lion, due to his strong leadership. And his precious mother was a seal, a happy seal—an annoyingly happy seal.

He must have really had it out for her. You just can't script this stuff.

While I don't exactly own the name Annoying, there are other names that I've embraced over the years. I've taken on names like:

> *Not Enough*
> *Unqualified*
> *Damaged*
> *Ugly*
> *Overwhelmed*

Maybe you carry names like that around too. Ever wanted to trade those names for a new name? I certainly have.

Tucked away in Revelation 2, Jesus promises, "I will give to each one a white stone, and on the stone will be engraved a new name that no one understands except the one who receives it" (verse 17).

A new God-given name engraved on a white stone? Sign me up.

Ancient Romans awarded white stones to the victors of athletic games. The champion of a contest was given a white stone with his name inscribed on it. This stone was his "ticket" to an awards banquet and earned the winner special privileges.

On a warm October day in Vegas, 650 women gathered at a conference ready to exchange their old names for new ones—the names they were created for. They held black river rocks in one hand and gold Sharpies in the other and made themselves vulnerable as they jotted their old names on the stones. They laid down old identities and traded them in for white stones of victory. An incredibly powerful moment.

A few days later, while the ladies traveled back home, my mom sat on the floor of my church surrounded by names written on black stones.

Good 4 Nothing
Bitter
Uninvited
Weak
Compromised
Fake
Selfish
Alone

She read stone after stone. She held each one in her hands and prayed for the woman who felt defined by that name. She felt compelled to help women ditch those old identities and find strength, freedom, and joy in who they were made to be. Thus, *My Name Is Victorious* was born.

Soon, we realized teens have adopted plenty of names of our own, too. We also have names that have haunted us, followed us, and held us back. We started creating a teen edition knowing that if we can learn now where the foundation of our identity lies, our lives can forever be changed.

As we dig into this workbook, we will grasp new names and embrace the fact that Jesus has declared us victors, overcomers, people worthy to be awarded a white stone.

Together, let's declare: "My name is Overcomer. My name is Conqueror. My name is Champion. My name is Victorious!"

How to Use and Abuse This Workbook

1. By the time you're done, this workbook will be marked up, messed up, and ripped up. Dog-ear the pages. Bend the spine. Throw it in your backpack with the crumbs and bubble gum wrappers. This book is meant to be used by you, not passed around to friends or resold in mint condition later. So tear into it. You can always duct-tape it back together later.

2. Dig deep. Do a little heart excavation. Grab a spade and shovel and really dig into your emotions, old wounds, fears, insecurities, and walls you've built around your heart. Don't rush; there are no blue ribbons for those who finish first. Take your time.

3. Be honest. No one has to know what is written inside—it's between you and God. When we are honest with ourselves about what's going on internally, God can really do a healing work. Truthfully, it's the best way to get the most out of the activities.

4. Speaking of the activities: Do them! Grab a pencil, a pen, some crayons, markers, or an inkwell and quill. Gather up your scissors and tape. We are going to get our arts and crafts on.

5. Don't forget—you are diving into this journal to expand your capacity to live well. Life is tough. We get it! We have some tough days and seasons too. But we can find strength, joy, and freedom in who He's created us to be.

6. Keep at it! See this through to the end. We've intentionally included twenty days of thought-provoking, hard-hitting, and practical content to explore. Do every last page.

7. Consider inviting someone along on the journey with you. Grab a friend and chat over coffee and chocolate croissants once a week. Hop on FaceTime with another pal so you can share your heart and your activities. Jump into a small group. Get knee to knee, eye to eye, and heart to heart with some kids at your church and dive into this workbook together. You'll find discussion questions tucked away throughout the book.

8. Watch the session videos as you move through the book. Get a jolt of encouragement in just a few minutes. Find the videos at **mynameisvictorious.com**

Take yourself on a coffee date. As you sip your latte, think about how you are feeling right this moment. How are you doing in these different areas of your life? Rank yourself on the latte scale. Color in the cups according to how full you feel in each area.

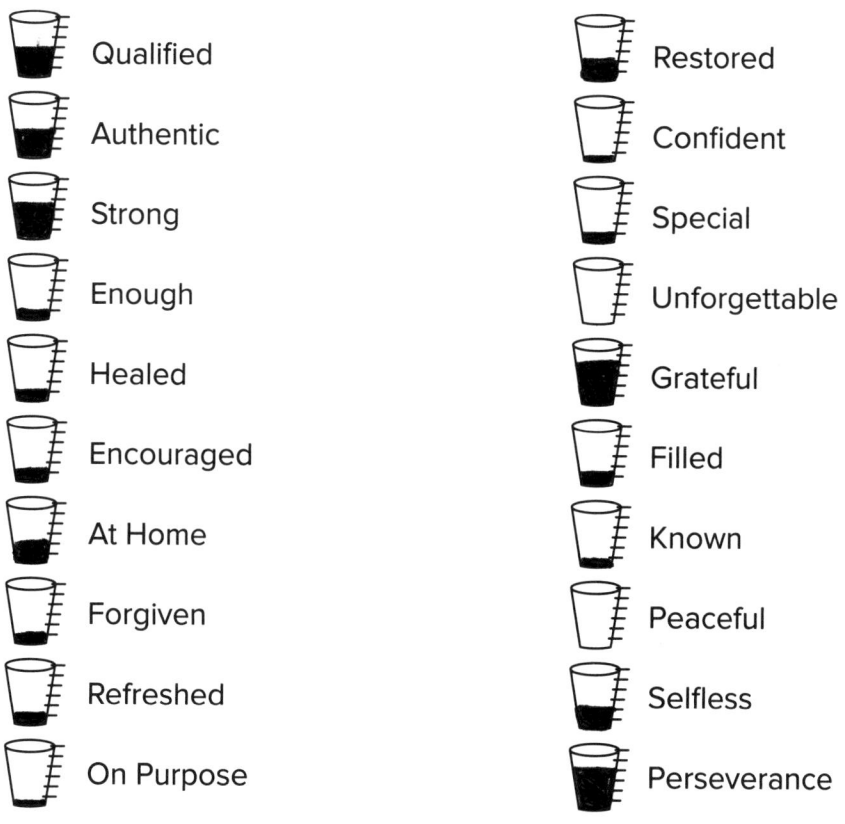

Qualified

Authentic

Strong

Enough

Healed

Encouraged

At Home

Forgiven

Refreshed

On Purpose

Restored

Confident

Special

Unforgettable

Grateful

Filled

Known

Peaceful

Selfless

Perseverance

On a good day, enjoy yourself;
On a bad day, examine your conscience.
God arranges for both kinds of days
So that we won't take anything for granted.
Ecclesiastes 7:14, MSG

Session 1

1. Unqualified

Some kids dream of becoming ballerinas. Others fantasize about being part of the Hollywood elite or YouTube famous. Still others imagine running down grassy fields and scoring touchdowns in professional football.

Not me. Nope.

When I was a little girl, I dreamed of becoming Rockstar Royalty. At my kindergarten graduation, each student was asked to stand up and announce what they wanted to be when they grew up. Some wanted to be police officers. Others professional tennis players. And one crazy kid claimed to be a future super spy. Ok kid. You're five. Relax.

When it was finally my turn, I confidently stood to my feet and declared, "I'm going to be the next American Idol!"

I visualized waiting in line for days with a paper number stuck to my stomach. I would finally get my moment in front of the judges. I would belt out an amazing Hannah Montana tune. I mean, I was five people. Hannah Montana was everything. And, of course, they would send me to Hollywood.

During Hollywood week, I would pick the perfect songs because song choice is key. When it was time for the group round, we would choreograph an incredible dance routine while singing in perfect pitch. We would all get along and stay up all night because we would never decide sleep was more important than practice. That would be the kiss of death. And on to the next round we would go.

When it was time to discover if I was named a finalist, I would walk down that long, lonely hallway with confidence. I wouldn't fall for it when the judges put on their sad faces and tried to make me feel like I was out. Their bait and switch wouldn't work on me! I would patiently wait for their, "... but you're going to be staying with us for a while since you are a finalist!"

On it would go. Week after week. Until the confetti would fall and my name was announced as the next American Idol. Yes. Rockstar Royalty, I tell you.

Others
- Stubborn
- annoying
- lazy
  ↳ - hardworking
    - Kind
    - funny

myself
- useless
- negative (swimming)
- Kind

Tape a picture (or draw one) of your kid self here. Look into those eyes. Check out that sweet smile. What did she think about? What did he dream of? What did she hope to become? Write those things in the thought bubbles below.

No matter what we dreamed of becoming one day, we all find ourselves in positions of influence now and in the future. Whether you lead at home, at school, or at church, ask yourself a single life-altering question: Am I God-commissioned?

Galatians 1:1 in The Message says: "My authority for writing to you does not come from any popular vote of the people, nor does it come through the appointment of some human higher-up. It comes directly from Jesus the Messiah and God the Father, who raised him from the dead. I'm God-commissioned."

You may feel strongly called to the role you're in now. God may have currently called you to be basketball player, a musical theater star, a STEM student, a master of debate, or a section leader in the school choir. He may be preparing you to accept His future call on your life. You may serve Him one day as a nurse, a high school principal, a real estate agent, or a restaurant manager. You may find yourself influencing three crazy toddlers at home or managing the staff at a retail store. Someday, you might be knee deep in leadership you never envisioned. You may even feel misplaced and confused by what your future looks like for you.

No matter how you find yourself in your place of influence, we believe you are God-commissioned.

None of us were called by popular vote. Take a stroll through our social media feeds, and you may find a long line of people not sending their votes our way. Whether they are leaving rude comments on your cute Instagram photos, spreading gossip about your family, or launching a full-scale attack campaign, we are all crystal clear that a popular vote didn't get us where we are today.

We didn't jump in by human appointment, including our own. We could fill journals with our lists of personal weaknesses and could easily drum up

101 shortcomings. We didn't appoint ourselves to these roles, because we know us. We doubt ourselves. And if we are gut-level honest, we doubt God's ability to use us. We doubt His ability to uniquely create us for the path He has laid out.

No. Not by popular vote. Not by our own appointment. We are God-commissioned. He chose us for these positions. He carefully placed us as influencers.

I AM GOD COMMISSIONED.

I am God Commisioned.
I am God Commissioned
I am God commissioned
I am God commissioned
I am God commissioned.
I am God commissioned.
I am God commissioned.
I am God commissioned.
I am God commissioned.
I am God commissioned

WE ARE HIS WORKMANSHIP, CREATED IN CHRIST JESUS FOR **GOOD** WORKS, WHICH **GOD PREPARED** BEFOREHAND, THAT WE SHOULD **WALK IN THEM.**

Ephesians 2:10, ESV

Hidden right at the end of 1 Chronicles 16 are thirteen little words that have the power to change our lives and leadership.

As King David returns the Ark of the Covenant, he walks among the people in the tent, assigning leadership roles. He chooses some to lead worship. Others he calls to play drums or trumpets. Still other men he assigns as security guards. And as David selects others, he adds these words: "...with the job description: 'Give thanks to God, for his love never quits!'" (1 Chronicles 16:41, MSG).

What if we—no matter our various roles now and in the future—were to fully live out the job description "Give thanks to God, for His love never quits"?

Are you a future kindergarten teacher? Your job description is: Give thanks to God, for His love never quits.

A future worship leader? Your job description is: Give thanks to God, for His love never quits.

A future shift manager? Your job description is: Give thanks to God, for His love never quits.

A future parent? Your job description is: Give thanks to God, for His love never quits.

A future small-group leader? Your job description is: Give thanks to God, for His love never quits.

A future physical therapist? Your job description is: Give thanks to God, for His love never quits.

A friend? Your job description is: Give thanks to God, for His love never quits.

Draw a new social media profile for yourself.
You have a brand new job:
**God Commissioned and
Giver of Thanks to God.**

We may feel ill-equipped. We may feel unqualified. We may feel that God has called us to do something we simply cannot do.

But we are fully capable of giving thanks to God, for His love never quits. We can let it seep deep down into our souls that we are God-commissioned, specially chosen, and specifically selected to do what He's called us to do. We may not feel qualified, but the Lord has deemed us so.

Today, embrace the fact that you—yes, you—are qualified.

Your new name is
QUALIFIED.
Declare it below!

MY NAME IS

Qualified

2. Damaged

One sunny spring day, a fellow popped into our church to talk with my dad. At the time, Dad was in a meeting with a family and wasn't available to connect. After declining a chance to chat with another pastor, the visitor left the building.

A few hours later, he reappeared, again asking to speak with my dad. Since it was one of those days chocked full of meetings and appointments, he wasn't available at the time. The offer to meet and pray with another pastor was again extended and refused, and the man left again.

Late in the afternoon, he returned to the church lobby. At that time, Dad was at an off-site meeting with a staff member. The guy was furious. He stormed off, only to reappear at three o'clock in the morning, when he drove his Toyota Corolla through the front doors of our church.

After doing a little demolition derby around the lobby, he drove his car down the hallways. He busted down fire doors, crashed into walls, and finally got his car stuck in a skinny back hallway. But not to worry—there was still more damage to be done. He climbed out of the car window, grabbing the large rocks he had brought with him. Those stones were perfect for putting holes in walls, busting the glass out of doors, and breaking video screens. As he rounded the corner back to the lobby, he was met by police officers and their Tasers.

We are now able to do drive-through weddings at our Vegas church.

Hopefully you haven't had someone drive their car through your church building. But we're willing to bet you've had someone do some demolition derby in your heart and life. You feel busted up, full of holes, damaged.

Who is in the driver's seat of the car that has damaged your heart and life? Draw them or write their name here.

Danielle

Recently, we read about the Japanese art of kintsugi, meaning "to patch with gold." When using the kintsugi technique, the artist takes broken ceramics or pottery and reassembles the pieces in an unusual way. Typically, restoration of damage is done so breaks are hidden and concealed, making the item as good as new. Kintsugi, however, uses precious metals such as gold and copper to reattach the shards and highlight the breaks instead of hiding them. The pottery becomes artistically better than new and can even become more valuable. Kintsugi is an art making broken things even more beautiful than before they were broken.[1]

Isn't that just like God?! He is in the business of healing hurts. He is the master at taking the broken pieces of our lives, restoring them, and making them even more beautiful than they've ever been. God made you, and He's got the perfect tools to fix whatever cracks you find. Because God loves using broken people just like you and me. Grace means all of our mistakes serve a purpose and not shame.

In my mere 17 years of life, I've had plenty of dings. Scratches due to criticism. Cracks caused by betrayal. Broken-off chunks as a result of my own mistakes. But I'm not damaged.

Dinged? Yes. Damaged? Not quite. I haven't been tossed in the damaged-goods box just yet.

When we've sustained a ding and wonder if we can bear to take one more, we remember that we have a choice before us. We can allow those dings to permanently damage and sideline us, or we can let God do His restoration work. It is as simple and as incredibly complicated as that.

Today, you may be dinged. But you don't have to be damaged. Not permanently.

Write the dings and damages you've endured into these cracks.

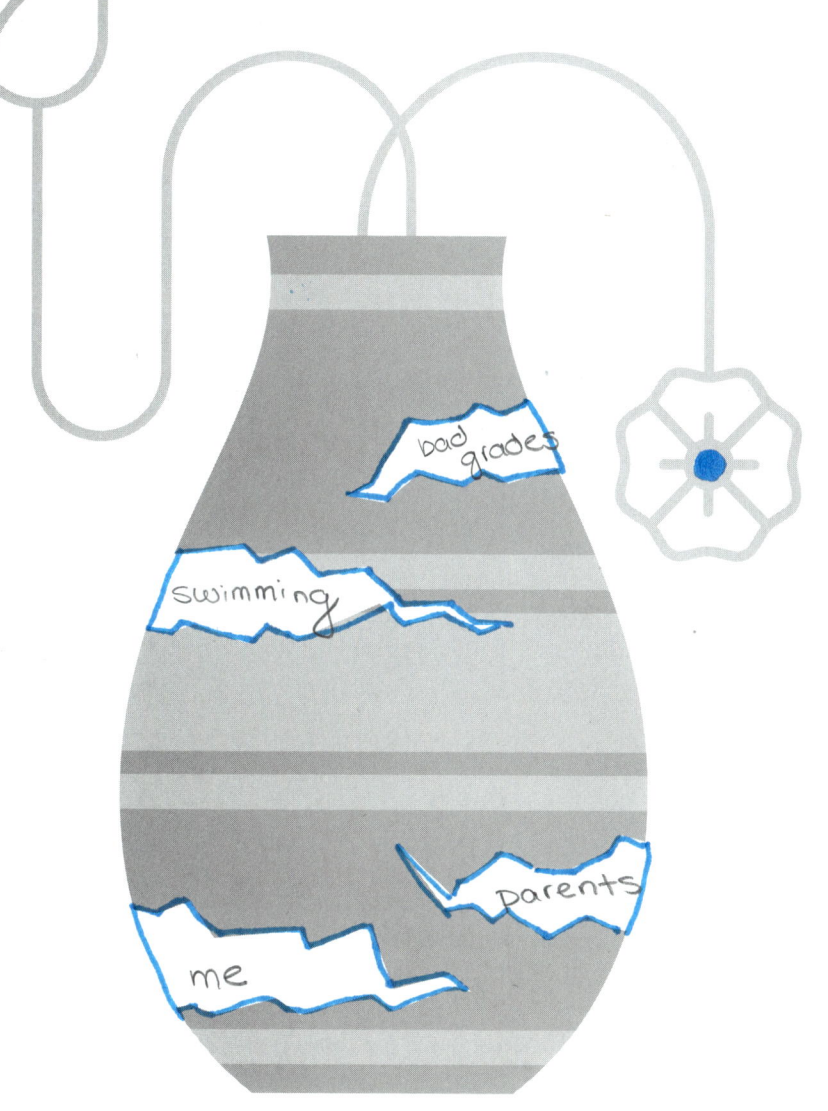

Now grab a gold, silver or copper crayon, and fill in the cracks. Let God make your brokenness beautiful.

Out of the dust we rise
Wonderfully made in the Savior's eyes
Created to shine the light
Through the broken-up pieces of my life

Shattered but not destroyed
Your cross was the bridge that filled the void
Living in Your grace, I'm overjoyed
And now I know, oh, oh

Your love goes higher, higher, sweeps me away
I'm drawing closer, closer every day
Sinking in deeper, deeper into Your grace
My life will never, ever be the same

I come alive again. I take a breath
My eyes open. I feel the pulse of my
Heart beating. Jesus has
Saved me. I'm feeling alive again

—"Alive Again" by Central Live

A desperate woman personally experienced Jesus and His incredible restoration work (Luke 8:43-48). We don't know if her name was Rebekah, Sarah, or Peggy Sue. We only know she is referred to as the bleeding woman. Twelve years of constant bleeding. Can you even imagine?! That's 4,380 days, or 105,120 hours, or 6,307,200 minutes of hemorrhaging. Unimaginable.

Deemed unclean and damaged, she sought out doctor after doctor. We can only imagine the horror she went through, give the state of medicine two thousand years ago. She spent every dime she owned, had her hope shattered, and still was no closer to a cure.

But then ... Jesus. With a throng of people pressing in around Him, Jesus walked by. I wonder if she had to lay prostrated on the dirt road reaching between the sandaled feet to touch the fringe of His robe. Or did she push herself between tightly packed bodies, frantically trying to stretch her arms enough so her fingertips would graze His hem?

By whatever means she grabbed hold of Jesus, in an instant she was healed. The power that leapt out of Jesus restored her damaged body and healed her brokenness. She was put back together in the most beautiful and extraordinary way!

Whatever your damage, no matter your brokenness, you can be made whole again.

Reach out to Jesus right now.
Stretch out and grab hold of Him.
Pour out your brokenness and ask for His healing.

Dear Jesus,

I'm having a hard time being myself. The confusion is causing me to lash out on the people I love the most, often. Help

Life isn't about being perfect. Not a single one of us is perfect. You don't have to be perfect! You just have to be willing. Willing to allow God to use your strengths and weaknesses to help others.

Please stop worrying about being perfect. Please! If there's one thing we know about ourselves, it's that we are not perfect. In fact, we don't believe we're supposed to be perfect. Each one of us has been positioned right here, right now, to be the person God created to make a difference in the lives of those around us. Our influence is not to promote perfection but to affirm authenticity. When we become vulnerable and authentic, we are saying to others it's okay to do the same. We're most effective when there's a genuineness that flows from our everyday lives. Many of us make a serious attempt to hide our imperfections, flaws, and mistakes. What would happen if we tore down the perfection platform and erected authenticity in its place? People are craving to see our real lives and the way we allow God to work in us and in our messes.[2]

If we are willing, God can use those imperfections and even our pain to bring more beauty into our own lives and to influence the lives of others.

This world is broken in so many ways, yet at the same time God is doing a fresh work! And He wants to do the same in you and me. He wants to take our failures, fears, and hurts and use them to make a difference.

Don't let your painful past, dings, cracks, and damage keep you out of the game. Press into Jesus and allow Him to heal you from the inside out. Then you will be a force to reckon with this side of heaven for His glory.

Your new name is
RESTORED.
Shout it out
below!

MY NAME IS

Restored

3. Impostor

One night as my mom lay in bed binge-watching her backed-up DVR, she was suddenly notified of a fake Facebook account using her name and information. Apparently this imposter was leaving reviews on our church's Facebook page. They said that my parents were seriously thinking of moving back to Texas and starting a church there since our church didn't take care of us. Whoa. Dang.

Seriously. "Fake Lori" is out there, people.

She proceeded to review several other churches in Vegas and beyond, always starting with "My husband Jud is the Senior Pastor at Central" and then absolutely decimating that ministry through nasty words and crazy insults.

As we scrambled to try to fix a mess before it became an absolute train wreck, it made us think.

One of the things we hold very highly is the abandoning of our fake selves. There is a great temptation to live behind a carefully crafted image, hiding our real selves so we can meet expectations or at least what we perceive as the expectations of others.

But that kind of impostor-living can only last so long. It is exhausting, and it will choke the joy out of life.

Instead, we can live joyfully in who God made us to be.

Compare and contrast. Be honest. Dig deep.

My social media self:

- Happy
- Athletic
- Pretty
- Confident

vs My Real Identity:

- Sad
- Weak
- Self concious

I am fascinated by *Catfish: The Documentary*.[3] It is the basis for one of my current binge-watch shows on MTV. In a crazy, convoluted story, poor Nev (the star of the show) becomes a pen pal with an eight-year-old artist named Abby. Nev eventually connects on Facebook with Abby's entire family: the mom Angela, dad, brother, and half-sister Megan. Nev and Megan start messaging online, then texting and talking, and falling for each other while never meeting in person. Over nine long months, they exchange over 1,500 messages containing many details about the family.

Angela has cancer. Lie.

Angela bought Abby an art gallery and is renovating it. Lie.

Abby's paintings sell for $7,000 each. Lie.

Megan looks like a supermodel. Lie.

Megan lives on a horse farm in Michigan. Lie.

Megan is writing and recording original songs. Lie.

Angela is, in fact, Megan and Abby and fifteen other people. True.

What. In. The. World?!

The web of deceit required to weave together the relationship between "Megan" and Nev was astounding. It took sixteen Facebook profiles, two cell phones, an obscene amount of time, and fake voices to create that web of lies.

With two special needs kids and unrealized dreams of what could have been, Angela wanted an escape from her life. She could be someone fake, an impostor. She could be someone new, more exciting.

Living a double life is exhausting. Let's be real for a second—it can be exhausting to live the one life we have! It is hard work to be yourself. It is double the work to invent a life and attempt to live that one as well.

Catfish is an extreme version of an impostor-self, but many of us do the same thing in small ways on a regular basis. We use a handy-dandy filter to make our selfies have thinner noses, brighter skin, and smoother faces. We answer "fine" when asked if we're okay, even though we are far from fine. We hide our pain behind pasted-on smiles and our hurt beneath happy social media captions. We try to be the people we think others want us to be. We keep our real selves tucked away so our friends won't be disappointed, our church family won't be scandalized, and the other kids at school won't look down their noses.

We're not suggesting we cease filtering our photos and cropping out dirty rooms in the background. We certainly won't be posting any #nomakeupmonday pictures anytime soon. But we can't lose ourselves. We have to find people with whom we can be our real selves.

It is time to drop the impostor. No masks. No fake. No phoniness.

Be you, no matter the location, situation, or audience watching—the same, real you in the halls at school, at Bible study on Wednesday night, at the after-school club meeting, in the discipleship group, at your little sister's soccer games, and at youth group on Sunday morning.

Just be you. The imperfect, yet uniquely gifted, authentic you.

Because God made you wonderfully. He gifted you uniquely. He placed certain passions in your heart. And He did not make a mistake with you.

I've spent a depressing number of years feeling like I needed to be someone else because I felt like I was lacking.

I am not an amazing performer like Taylor Swift. I am not an inspiring author like J.K. Rowling or even my dad. I am not an incredible songwriter like Ed Sheeran. The list could go on and on.

Great news! God already has a Taylor Swift and Ed Sheeran. He is already moving through J.K. Rowling and Jud Wilhite. So I don't have to be like them! I can be the one and only me. And you can be the one and only you.

God created you for a special purpose, and you can be the best, realest you possible. Push the impostor aside. Today, rest in who God has created you to be.

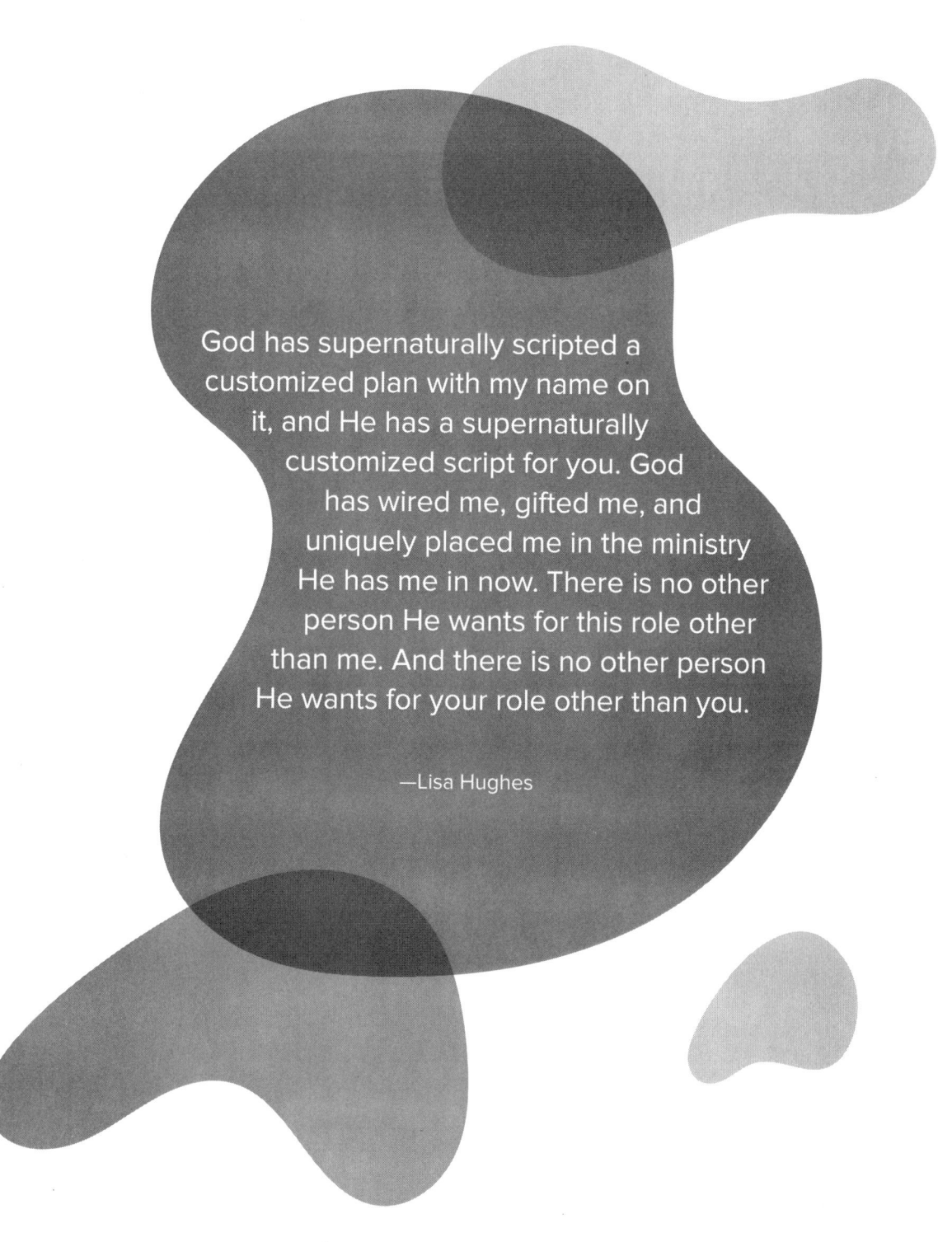

God has supernaturally scripted a customized plan with my name on it, and He has a supernaturally customized script for you. God has wired me, gifted me, and uniquely placed me in the ministry He has me in now. There is no other person He wants for this role other than me. And there is no other person He wants for your role other than you.

—Lisa Hughes

Oh to be a super hero, with a golden lasso and
bulletproof bracelets.

If you could have super powers, what would you wish for?

You may not be a super hero, but you have unique
God-given gifts! List them below.

SUPER
POWERS

* * * * * * *

GOD-GIVEN
GIFTS

* * * * * * *

The book of Acts lays out the story of two master fakers, Ananias and Sapphira. Having sold some land, the couple conspire to hide some of their dough but pretend they are gifting the entire income from the sale to the church. They weren't required to give their newly obtained money away, but with a little bit of deception and a truckload of hypocrisy, Ananias showed up to declare that the full amount was being offered.

Big mistake. Big.

The apostle Peter locks eyes with the man trying to fake his way to favor and says, "Ananias, why have you let Satan fill your heart? You lied to the Holy Spirit, and you kept some of the money for yourself. The property was yours to sell or not sell, as you wished. And after selling it, the money was also yours to give away. How could you do a thing like this? You weren't lying to us but to God!" (Acts 5:3-4)

Essentially he says: Hey, dude. You didn't just show up here today and lie to us, but you flat-out lied to God. You could have done whatever you wanted with that money. Instead, you stand here, a complete phony, lying to the Holy Spirit. Seriously?! What were you thinking?

Then Ananias falls over and dies. Right there.

But that's not all. Three hours later his fraudulent wife shows up to meet with the apostles as well. Here's her chance to own it, to be the real deal. When Peter asks if that is the full amount she and Ananias received, she quickly affirms what her husband claimed.

Not good. Not good at all.

A few minutes later, she is carried out to be buried next to her husband.

Whoa. Those are some serious consequences when it comes to lying, deceiving, and faking. While we may not keel over when we kick the true versions of ourselves to the curb while promoting our fake-selves instead, that kind of deception can still have serious consequences.

You can't fake your way to favor. Oh, sure, you might be able to for a time. But eventually the jig will be up. Because our phony selves aren't just lying to people but lying to God. Why would we lie to the Lord when He fully knows our authentic selves anyway? Pointless.

It's time to leave the imposter behind.
Embrace the real you and live authentically.
Draw your self-portrait below. Your real self.
You don't have to be literal. Don't overthink it.
Just go for it.

woo!

Your new name is
AUTHENTIC.
Proudly write it
below!

MY NAME IS

Authentic

4. Insecure

There are a few sayings that can send chills down my spine. They are that terrifying.

First: "Emma, clean your room!" ... Pure terror strikes when I hear those words. No thanks, I'll just continue in my filth.

Next: "Look nice because your cousins are coming over." ... aka time to finally emerge from my room, change out of my pajamas, and speedily rip a hairbrush through my hair. Is it obvious I'm not a "morning person" or a "do anything that requires moving" person?

Last: "I had to plug my ears. Your singing/screaming was so loud."

Yep. Those words were spoken to me the very first time I led a worship song in our main auditorium at church. In the moment, I laughed and jokingly apologized, yet the words hung around. They echoed in my ears causing me to heap additional pressure on myself for years. Those words brought out my deepest insecurities.

It became more and more difficult to do what I loved without constant self doubt. That ever present doubt came with a list of weaknesses, faults, and failures making me want to quit. I couldn't come up with any attributes that could make me feel worthy to lead worship. Instead I was stuck with a five-hundred-pound backpack full of insecurity that wore me out and pulled me down.

Surely I am not the only person who has carried insecurity and lugged around doubt.

What's in your backpack?
What weighs you down?
Write those things below.

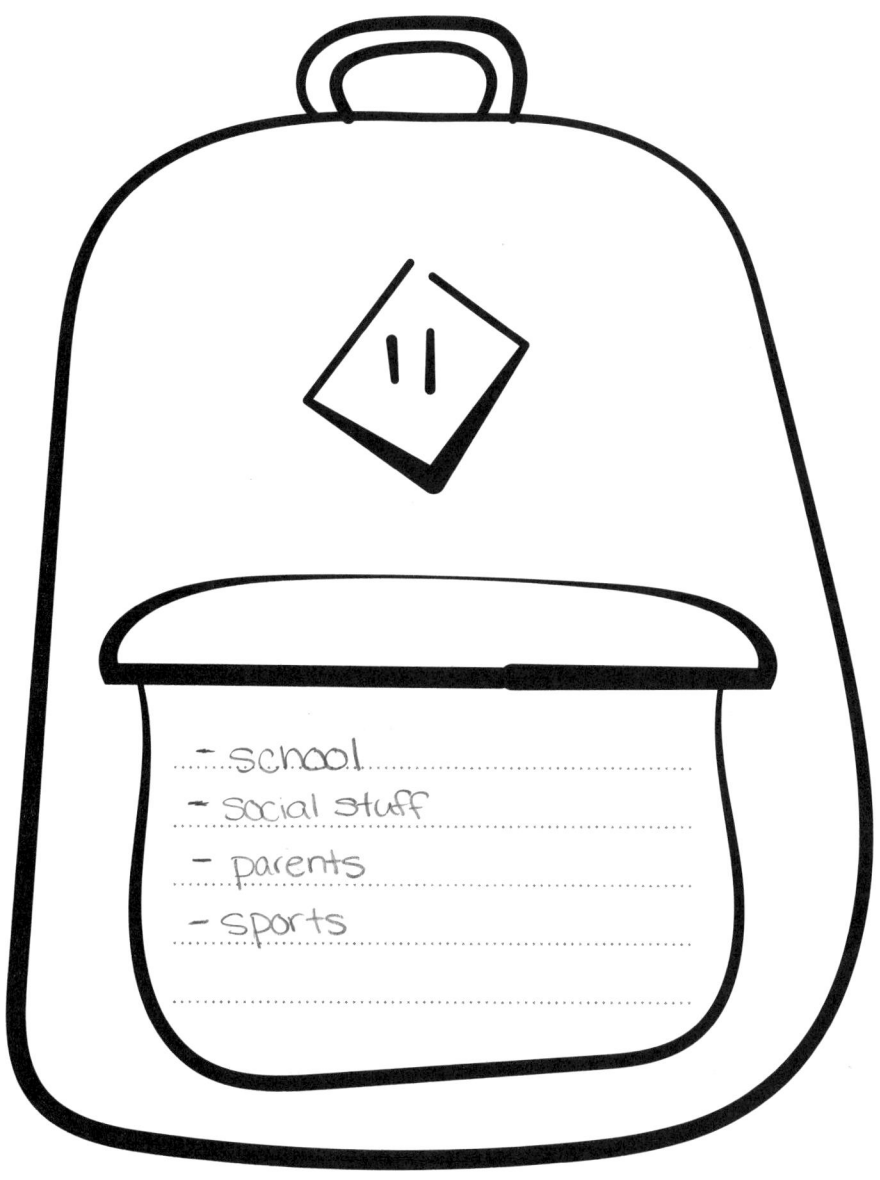

- school
- social stuff
- parents
- sports

We know we're not the only ones lugging around a knapsack full of insecurity. Just flip over to Exodus 3, and we'll see a leader who was overwhelmed with his calling and the terror that he might not be the right man for the job—that he might totally mess it up. In just a few verses, God lays out His plan for Moses's life (He would lead God's people to freedom), and Moses protests that calling with a litany of excuses.

Who am I?

How can I lead?

They won't believe me.

I'm not a good speaker.

Send someone else.

I'm not good enough.

I'm not equipped.

I'm not qualified.

I'm not gifted.

There are so many others better than me.

Oh, Moses. I get you. I surely do.

Then he's met with these powerful words: "I am who I am. Say this to the people of Israel: I am has sent me to you" (verse 14, NIV).

The One who is sovereign. The One who is all-knowing. The One who is all-powerful. The One who is so much bigger than any teeny-tiny box you might try to fit Me in. You tell them, I AM chose you, called you, sent you.

We, too, have protested God's call: I'm not good enough. I'm not equipped. I'm not qualified. I'm not gifted. There are so many others better than me.

One day, my mom grabbed me by the shoulders and asked, "Do you believe God is sovereign? Do you think He knows what He's doing?"

Yes. Duh. Of course He's sovereign. Of course He knows what He's doing.

My mom looked me in the eyes and asked, "Then do you not believe that God knew exactly what He was doing when He chose you? Do you not believe that God knows exactly who He wants to lead people in worship? Do you not believe that God knows the worship pastor your future church will need? Do you not believe He is sovereign?"

Whoa. Deep breath. Take a step back.

Yeah. We do. We do believe He's sovereign. Even though we feel like we're not equipped, qualified, or gifted enough. Even though we know there are so many other incredible people out there. Even though we worry we might mess everything thing up. We will rest in the knowledge that we are chosen.

And so are you.

THE CALLING ON YOUR LIFE
IS DIRECTLY FROM GOD.
He chose you.

HE DETERMINES YOUR
PURPOSE.

—Linda Seidler

Let me grab you by the shoulders and ask you the same question.

DO YOU BELIEVE GOD IS SOVEREIGN?
Circle **YES** or **NO.**

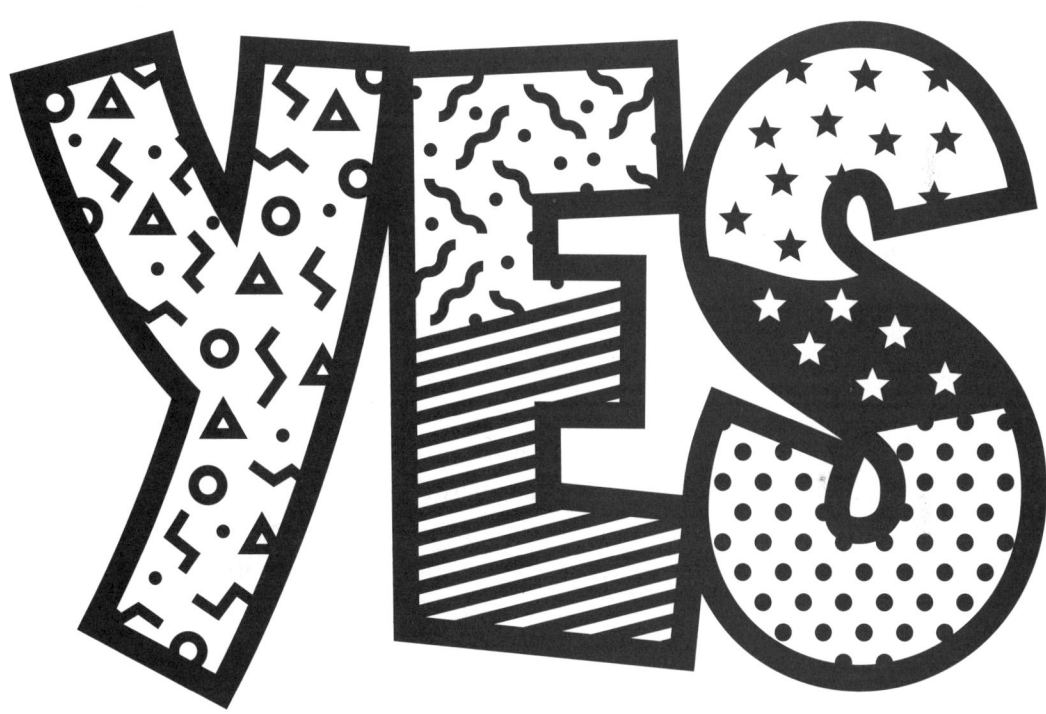

NO

When we realize we are chosen, confidence begins to follow. But who is the confident person really? And do I have what it takes to be completely confident in who God has called me to be?

We've often wondered that. We bet you have too.

For most of us, the word confident evokes the image of people who have it all together. They don't struggle with self-doubt. They know their purpose. They don't question their calling. They are secure in themselves. They can handle all life throws their way. They effortlessly manage their schedules. The list goes on.

While most of us may see this as the image of a confident person, this is not the reality within a confident person.

You see, a confident person knows their confidence does not come from what they accomplish or their calmness in a tense situation. They are assured that who they are does not depend on how many trophies they accumulate or how many A's they get on their report card.

A confident person makes it apparent that the level of your confidence runs parallel to your dependence on God. It is not based on your performance level. A confident person understands that the imperfection in your life encourages you to rely on God to fill the places where you lack. You know all temporal things on this earth will change, and because the great I am never changes, you can be secure and confident in who you are because of who He is.

Proverbs 3:26 (NASB) says, "The Lord will be your confidence."

Did you see that? God is your source of confidence! He will give you the confidence you need! It's called God-fidence, and it's critical for you and me to start believing what He says about us. We can't depend on what others say, nor the unachievable expectations we place on ourselves. When we allow God to be our source of confidence, we can stop the cycle of suffering through a lifetime of doubt and uncertainty in our personal lives, families, and relationships.

So you may be wondering if there is anyone who really carries the mantle of confidence every day. Is this confidence possible for me?

The answer is: Yes! But many times, we have our ear tuned in more to a deceitful enemy, who wants to tear us down, instead of our mighty God, who wants to build us up.

Take a look at the following truths in God's Word and invite God to strengthen your heart, soul, and mind to believe what He says.[4]

Because of the great I AM, you can have confidence today that:

> You are chosen (Ephesians 1:4-5).

> You are qualified (2 Corinthians 3:5).

> You can do all things through Christ who strengthens you (Philippians 4:13).

> God has equipped, gifted, and purposed you for great things (Hebrews 13:20-21).

> You are accepted (Colossians 1:21-22).

> God is preparing within you what He has prepared for you (Ephesians 2:10).

> You are forgiven (1 John 1:9).

You are an overcomer (Romans 8:37).

You are saved by His mercy (Titus 3:4-5).

You are never alone (Hebrews 13:5).

You are uniquely made (Psalm 139:14).

You are unconditionally loved and eternally bound to God (Romans 5:8).

You have what it takes and are more than enough (Ephesians 1:17-18).

You are redeemed (Ephesians 1:7).

Your former shame has no power in your present (Isaiah 50:7).

You are wonderful (Psalm 139:14).

You are strong, and God has armed you with the power to get through obstacles you face (Isaiah 40:28-31).

You're more then what you think you are. Stop comparing yourself to other people, you arent them. Stop relying on other people to determine your worth. Do what makes you happy, not what makes your parents happy.

God is not sorry He chose us. He's not sorry He chose you. In fact, He's chosen each of us to do something of profound impact. We will not allow fear to sideline us, to paralyze us from doing what we've been chosen to do. We are not on this journey alone. He has prepared our paths. God chose you! As Paul says in Galatians 1:15, "Even before I was born, God chose me and called me by his marvelous grace."

Your new name is
CONFIDENT.
Claim it below!

MY NAME IS

Confident

5. Weak

One painfully early Saturday morning, my youth leadership group from church decided to set out on a huge hike in the mountains surrounding Las Vegas. Now going into this I naively thought, "How bad could it be? I mean, sure, I haven't done any physical activity in like two years, but surely, it's all good!" Wrong!

The hike immediately started uphill, and I quickly knew I was in trouble. My friend, Faith, and I not-so-confidently held up the back of the pack the entire hike. There was one instance where some brainiac decided it was a good idea to go off the trail, leading us to climb a steep slope covered with loose gravel to get back on track. After losing my footing several times, I was growing weary of seeing my life flash before my eyes. After one of the guys had to drag me up the slope, I realized how incredibly weak I was as I dramatically panted and stumbled around.

If it wasn't clear then, it was definitely clear the next day when I could barely move a muscle following our little hiking adventure. I was weak. W-E-A-K! Like not-able-to-move-my-legs-the-next-day kind of weak.

Later I realized I tend to do this a lot in life. I look at the path ahead and I think, "It can't be that bad. I'm pretty strong, I've got this!"

Then I get smack dab in the middle and realize, I'm not quite as strong as I thought. The steps I take get harder and harder, and my breathing gets heavier and heavier. What should be easy seems much more difficult the weaker I feel.

Draw muscles on the kids below to describe how strong or weak you are feeling right now.

Physically

Mentally

Emotionally

Spiritually

We are pitiful runners. We managed to hit the finish line of a 5k thanks to some pretty fabulous wogging. Yep, wogging. Walking + jogging = wogging. If we're honest, it was way more of the former than the latter.

We can't even imagine the fatigue and weakness that sets in during a marathon. Take this article from Newsday that looks at what happens to your body in the middle of a marathon:

> Although it varies by runner, many marathoners say they "hit the wall" somewhere in the 15- to 20-mile range of the race. At this point, you've probably built up a lot of lactic acid in your body, your legs are locking up and your electrolytes and phosphorus levels may also be low. And you're starting to get fatigued...
>
> You're more than halfway through and yet you still have a 10K to go as you cross the 20-mile marker. If you haven't hit the "wall" yet, you're probably close to smacking into it at this point.[5]

Ever feel like you've smacked straight into the proverbial wall? That you are so fatigued your brain is in a fog? That you've taken a huge beating? That you feel so weak you can't keep going?

All of that makes Isaiah 40:29-31 even more incredible:

> He gives power to the weak
>   and strength to the powerless.
> Even youths will become weak and tired,
>   and young men will fall in exhaustion.
> But those who trust in the Lord will find new strength.
>   They will soar high on wings like eagles.
> They will run and not grow weary.
>   They will walk and not faint.

We love the progression of this passage. Who wouldn't want to spread their wings and soar? Everyone would love to run and not grow weary. But the last bit is our favorite. We will walk and not faint. As much as we think God delights in soaring and running, we wonder if He's most pleased with those who choose the strength to walk.

When our legs feel like lead. When we don't have muscle to put one foot in front of the other. When we can't summon up the energy to take another step, we trust in the Lord and find a new strength.

We embrace the strength to keep moving those legs forward. We grab hold of the strength to put one foot in front of the other. We tap into the strength to take one more step. We keep walking.

When we are at our weakest, God gives us power and strength. All of us, every single one, will have times when we may feel weak and tired, but keep trusting in the Lord! By continually trusting in Him, we won't grow weak, weary, or faint.

What is
ONE NEXT STEP
you can take today in God's power?
Write that step below.

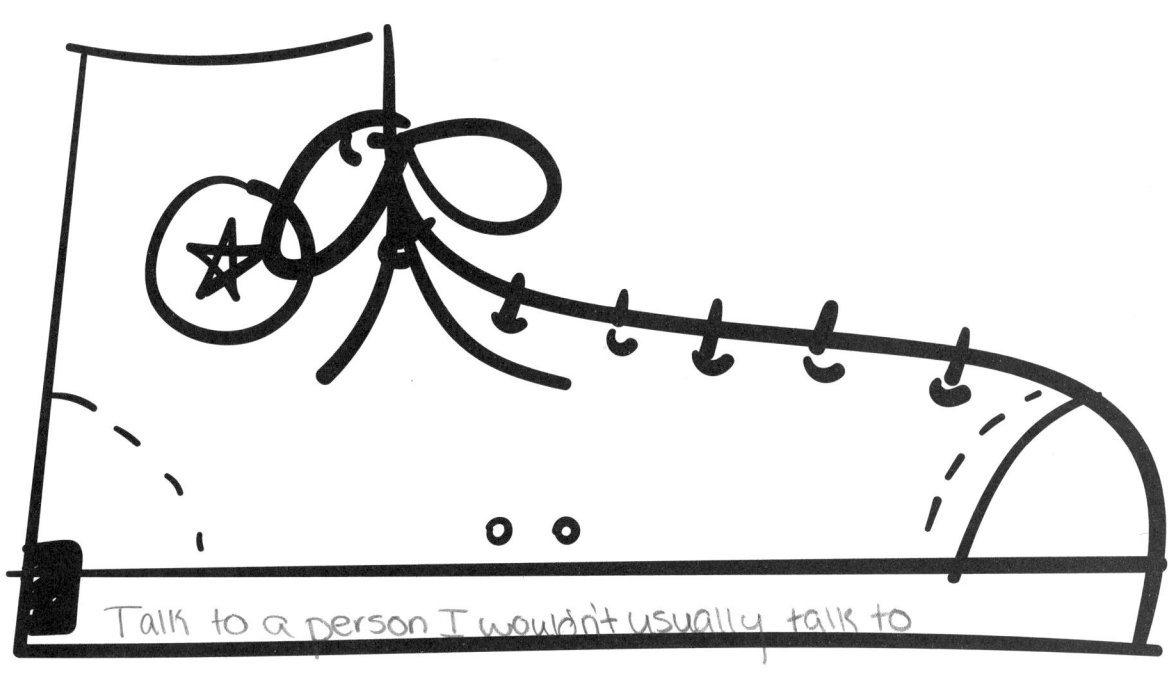

Talk to a person I wouldn't usually talk to

MY SOUL IS WEARY

WITH SORROW;

strengthen me

ACCORDING TO

YOUR WORD.

—PSALM 119:28, NIV

Life is a funny thing. It can be absolutely exhilarating or incredibly grueling. Usually it is both—at the same time. The pressures of life, the cares of people, the responsibilities we shoulder, and the balancing act we manage daily can leave us occasionally depleted of strength. There is no greater way to renew our strength than the Word of God!

> "He [the Lord] said, 'My grace is all you need. My power works best in weakness.' So now I am glad to boast about my weaknesses, so that the power of Christ can work through me. That's why I take pleasure in my weaknesses, and in the insults, hardships, persecutions, and troubles that I suffer for Christ. For when I am weak, then I am strong." (2 Corinthians 12:9-10)

When we feel weak, it's a perfect opportunity to allow God's strength to work in and through us. We can gladly recognize our weaknesses so the Lord can turn them into strengths in our lives. We can willingly embrace our weaknesses so we can become strong in Christ.

> God is our refuge and strength,
>   always ready to help in times of trouble. (Psalm 46:1)

That's right, God is always ready to help us. Many times we encounter situations intended to weaken us. Even though we might not be prepared to handle them, they are no surprise to our heavenly Father. He was ready before the problem even showed up. He's ready to help us overcome!

> Those who live in the shelter of the Most High
>   will find rest in the shadow of the Almighty.
> This I declare about the Lord:
> He alone is my refuge, my place of safety;
>   He is my God, and I trust him. (Psalm 91:1-2)

God is also our refuge. He is the place we run to for protection, safety, and shelter from the storms of life. When we run to Him, we find rest and peace.

> The Lord is my strength and shield.
> I trust him with all my heart.
> He helps me, and my heart is filled with joy.
> I burst out in songs of thanksgiving. (Psalm 28:7-8)

Thankfully, we don't always have to be strong; we can rely on His strength in our lives. Once we realize that any strength we have comes only from Him, it will become easier to truly trust Him instead of looking to ourselves for strength when we are weak. When we recognize the Lord is our strength, joy fills our hearts.

Nehemiah 8:10 says, "Don't be dejected and sad, for the joy of the Lord is your strength!"

The joy that fills our hearts when we realize the Lord is our strength sustains our strength. Strength comes from the joy of the Lord and overrides any weakness we may feel![6]

GOD IS OUR REFUGE AND STRENGTH, ALWAYS READY TO HELP IN TIMES OF TROUBLE.

Psalm 46:1

THOSE WHO LIVE IN THE **SHELTER** OF THE **MOST HIGH** WILL FIND **REST** IN THE SHADOW OF THE ALMIGHTY. HE **ALONE** IS MY **REFUGE,** MY PLACE OF **SAFETY;** HE IS MY GOD, AND I TRUST HIM.

Psalm 91:1-2

Read these verses. Cut them out and place them where you will see them daily. Start committing these Scriptures to memory so you will be strengthened by His Word.

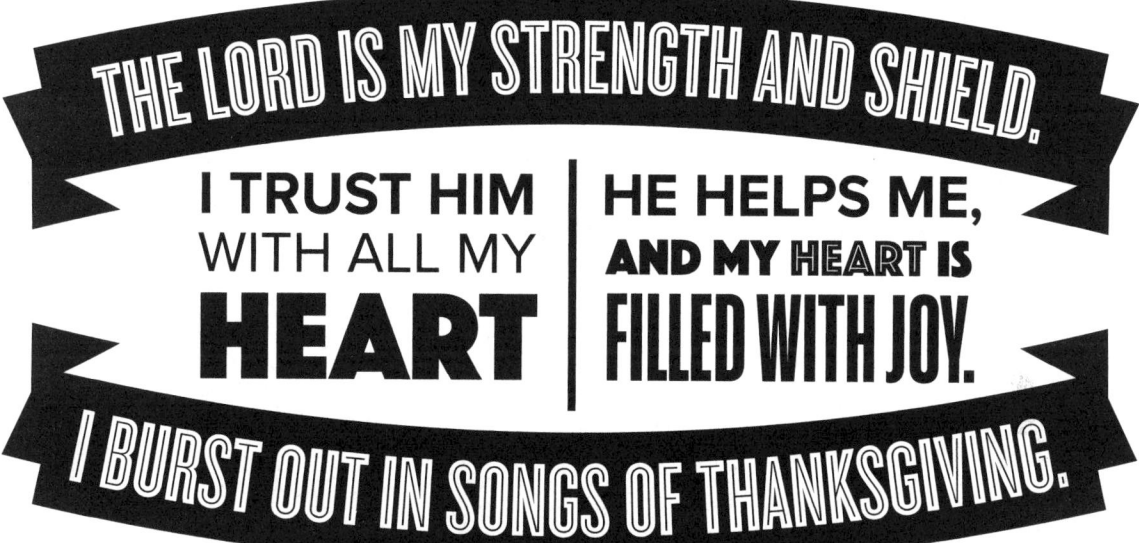

THE LORD IS MY STRENGTH AND SHIELD.

I TRUST HIM WITH ALL MY HEART

HE HELPS ME, AND MY HEART IS FILLED WITH JOY.

I BURST OUT IN SONGS OF THANKSGIVING.

Psalm 28:7-8

DON'T BE DEJECTED AND SAD,

FOR THE JOY OF THE LORD IS YOUR STRENGTH!

Nehemiah 8:10

Your new name is **STRONG.** Announce it with trumpets and streamers below!

MY NAME IS

STRONG

Group Discussion Questions

1. What did you dream about becoming when you were a kid? What role has God commissioned you for today?

2. We've all experienced damage in our hearts or lives. Share one crack or ding you've sustained.

3. Is your social media self an accurate reflection of your real self? Describe the similarities and differences.

4. What kind of insecurities fill the backpack you haul around? How can you unpack that insecurity to make room for more confidence?

5. How strong (or weak) are you feeling physically, mentally, emotionally, spiritually? Why?

Session 2

6. Not Special

Growing up I never thought myself special. I instead strove to make myself seem special in the eyes of my friends and the people around me.

I tended to think of myself as a "chameleon" wearing other people's personalities in order to seem more likable. I changed my colors because I was afraid I would never be special enough. Eventually, I could not even recognize myself. I had forgotten who I really was.

Social media made it easy to compare myself to others. I wanted to be more like the perfect and carefree people I saw on Instagram - not realizing that posts only captured a well-filtered moment, not reality. It took a long time to realize that the friends I might gain as my "chameleon" self wouldn't truly love me for me. Instead they would only know the image I projected to them.

If we aren't careful, we can lose ourselves in the comparison game. Comparison is the internal measuring tape we carry in our back pocket. We use it to measure our deficiencies against the best qualities we see in others, and we fall short. Or we pull it out to measure our successes against the weaknesses of someone else, and we fly high.

Neither of these is how God wants us to see ourselves.

If we allow it residence, comparison will occupy and fill space in our minds with thoughts that limit our potential and hold us back. It's almost as if we lock ourselves into a way of thinking that is contrary to how God designed us. We are literally caught in the comparison trap.

Let's take a look at some truths about comparison and how we can become free from its grip.

People I compare myself to...
even though
I know I **SHOULDN'T.**

X Celebrities
_____

X my friends
_____

X my family members
_____

X girls smarter than me
_____

X girls more athletic than me
_____

I'LL CALL **NOBODIES** AND MAKE THEM **SOMEBODIES.** I'LL CALL THE **UNLOVED** AND MAKE THEM **BELOVED.**

IN THE PLACE WHERE THEY YELLED OUT, "YOU'RE NOBODY!" **THEY'RE CALLING YOU "GOD'S LIVING CHILDREN."**

—ROMANS 9:25-26, MSG

There is one and only one you in all of time, and that, my friend, is pretty special! Your expression is unique, and you have something that no one else has—your mind, your voice, your talents, your abilities, your vision, your story. The list goes on.

But instead of looking at everything God has made each of us to be, we can get laser-focused on the achievements and talents of someone else. That can lead to hating ourselves for everything we are not, instead of loving ourselves for everything we are. We become jealous, bitter, and withdrawn and eventually stop what we started because we doubt our self-worth and think we aren't good enough.

You can't stop your expression! If you do, the world will be without something fabulous that God intended for it to have, and that's you.[7]

So remind yourself of how God adoringly made you a unique creation filled with wonder and awe. He approached even the smallest detail with excellence. You are wonderful.

God made you to be you, and the world needs you to do what only you can do. You are truly like no other person ever created since time began. You are incomparable.

What is special about you?
Write all of the wonderful things about
you that help you bloom. Don't stop
until every petal is filled with how God
made you a unique creation.

caring

smart

hardworking

nice

loving

passionate

I like racing

kind of funny

genuine

talkative

good leader

We love this quote—"A flower doesn't compare itself with the flowers around it. It just blooms." This is God's ultimate design for us. Be like the flower that can bloom and thrive and be incredible alongside other flowers that are blooming and thriving and being incredible.

God created all of us in His image with distinct differences and unique talents and giftings, yet we work alongside one another to function as the one body of Christ. We lock arms with one another and admire the accomplishments and achievements each other contributes. God has designed us to work together, cheer each other on, and believe in each other. This is a healthy component and necessary part of functioning well within the body of Christ.

What is not healthy? Being tempted to intentionally withhold encouragement from someone who is doing well. Okay, just press Pause for a minute and take an honest look to make sure you are not internally comparing. Remind yourself that someone else's doing well will not take away from your doing well. And it most certainly doesn't mean that you are not gifted or talented.

Just because he is good at writing doesn't mean you are not. Just because she sings like an angel doesn't mean you sound hideous. Just because they are talented, have a great family, and are on the honor roll and thriving does not mean you have a life that is lesser than that!

It just means you are two different people. Truly, that's all it means.

So decide to celebrate with those whom you admire, and celebrate big! 1 Thessalonians 5:11 (NIV) says it best: "Encourage one another and build each other up."[8]

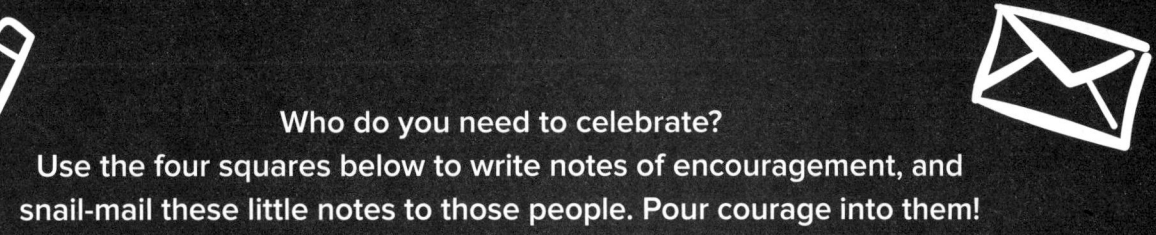

Who do you need to celebrate?
Use the four squares below to write notes of encouragement, and
snail-mail these little notes to those people. Pour courage into them!

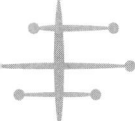

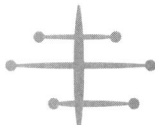

Last, focus on your own dreams and ambitions. When we compare, we are giving more attention to another person's achievements than we are to our own.

Ask yourself, what and who am I focusing on? What are my goals? What do I want my future to look like? What kinds of relationships am I aspiring to have? How has God equipped me to move ahead? Does what I am striving for fall under God's will for me?

Remember, you have not been called to be like someone else. You have been called to be like Jesus. So stop comparing your life to another's, and start focusing your thoughts on Jesus.

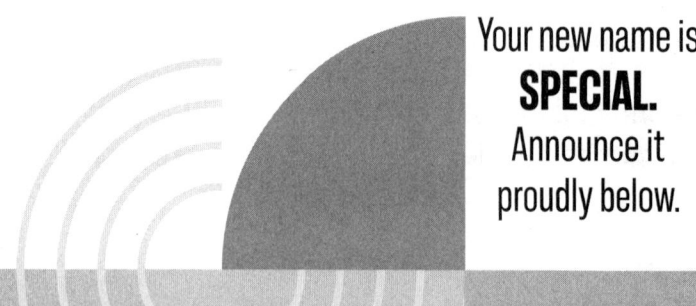

Your new name is
SPECIAL.
Announce it
proudly below.

MY NAME IS

SPECIAL

7. Not Enough

Going to a college-prep school filled with competitive, smart kids can be very stressful. Watching the students around me easily excel while my immense effort just barely gets me to the "A" mark, takes a toll on me. The question I fear the most is one of the other kids asking, "What's your school ranking?" Whether at the bottom or at the top, the stress still remains. My boundless effort to try to climb my way up the academic ladder leaves me feeling like I'm just simply not enough.

I've always known my grades were good, but they're not enough. My parents have told me time and time again that my grades were great and that they are proud of me. But all I hear is the echoes reverberating in my mind that they just aren't "good enough." My 3.9 GPA pushes me out of the top quarter of my class. It keeps me from attending awards ceremonies. But I do get a form letter from my principal, so there's that. Comparing myself to my smarty-pants, 4.1, STEM, best friends leaves me feeling pathetic despite my achievements.

I am notoriously hard on myself. I constantly feel like I should be this, I should do that, I should be better, I should do more. I should, I should, I should. I can't seem to stop "shoulding" myself.

Yes, I must continue to grow and strive to be a better person. But I also need to try to rest in my security in Christ and see myself more like He sees me.

Are you "shoulding" yourself, too?

CONFESSION TIME

What makes you not-enough? What do you do that you feel like you shouldn't? Or what do you not do that you feel like you should?

I'll go first:

I should stop obsessively binge watching Netflix.

I shouldn't dive down the rabbit hole of the Instagram Explore page for hours on end.

Your turn:

I feel not enough because my friends are smarter than me.

I should stop procrastinating. It makes me SAD!

Just another one of those days busy trying to finish odds and ends. We struggle to find something to wear amongst the stained and hole-filled shirts in our closets. We pick up all of our devices and junk that have found a home on the floor even though we know they will magically reappear in the next five minutes. We are bored at home on a Friday night and end up mindlessly watching YouTube videos.

Then we pop open social media. Big mistake. We normally enjoy viewing photos and reading posts by family, friends, and people we like to pretend are friends. Social media has invaded not only our phones but—dare we say— also our hearts.

We see friends in their spotless, freshly pressed, fashionable outfits. We notice homes that look like they popped out of magazines. And we behold photo after photo of people out having a blast on their Friday night.

Have you noticed that while regarding others you find yourself scrutinizing or, more often than not, criticizing? You not only observe others, but you label them and at the same time label yourself. You think:

> *She is such a pretty model. I haven't even brushed my hair today!*
> *I can't cook like that. I even burned my pizza rolls.*
> *Her room is immaculate. My room looks like it was hit with a tornado.*
> *I haven't visited those fabulous destinations. My life is so boring!*
> *My posts on Instagram are not as spiritual as those. Something must be wrong with my faith.*
> *Look at those people enjoying a night out. I am alone. I don't have friends.*

Instead of feeling joy and happiness for friends, the information overload produces a sense of comparison as we constantly think that we are not good enough. Our vision of life is reduced to thinking about the things we lack. How we don't quite measure up.

The comparison game starts to take root in our lives.

But in the comparison game, there are no winners. Comparison kills contentment.

Atelophobia

The fear of imperfection.
The fear of never being good enough.

Take a look in the mirror. What are some areas of your life where comparison has killed your contentment? Write them in the mirror below.

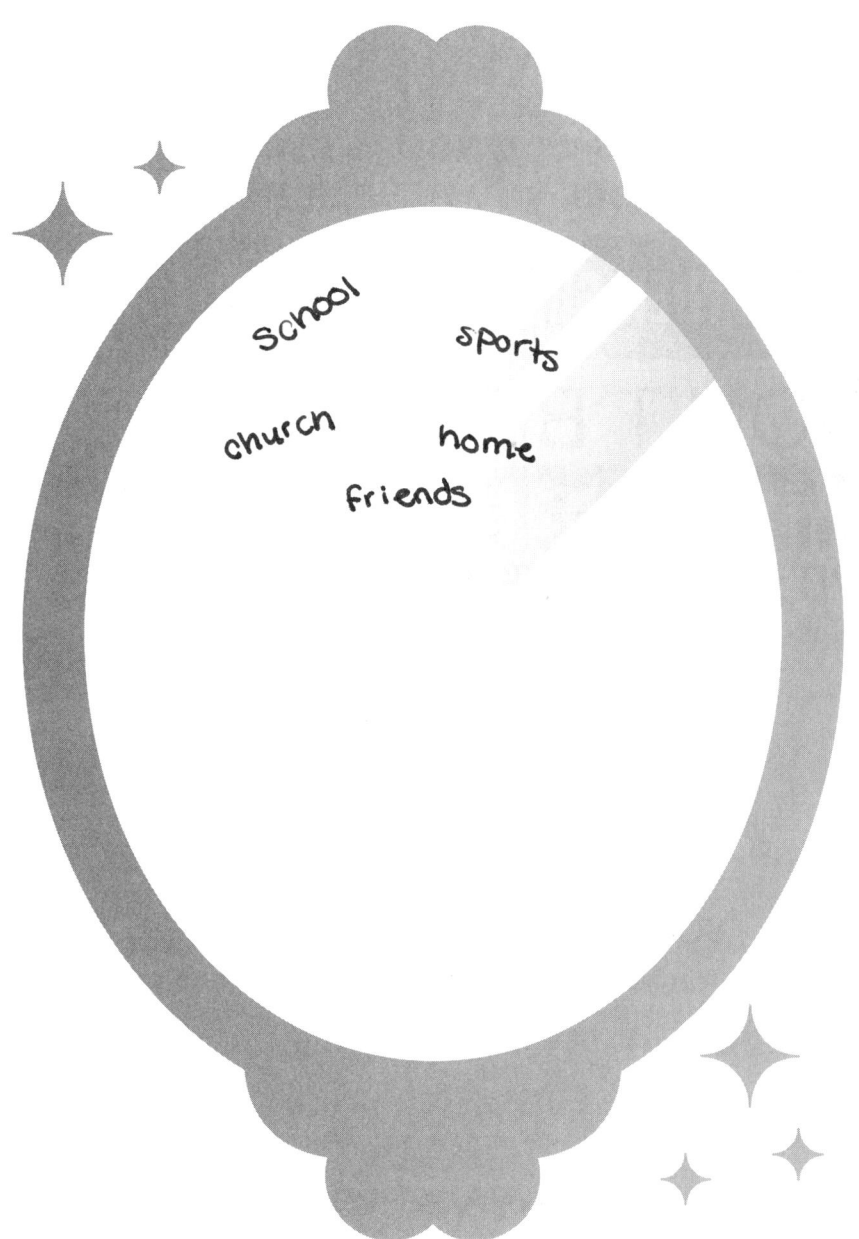

School

sports

church

home

friends

MAKE A

careful exploration

OF WHO YOU ARE AND
THE WORK YOU HAVE BEEN GIVEN,

AND THEN SINK YOURSELF INTO THAT.

DON'T BE
IMPRESSED
WITH YOURSELF.

DON'T **COMPARE**
YOURSELF WITH
OTHERS.

EACH OF YOU MUST TAKE
RESPONSIBILITY FOR DOING THE

creative best

YOU CAN WITH YOUR OWN LIFE.

—Galatians 6:4-5, MSG

When my mom was in junior high, there was one sure-fire, incredibly impactful way to let someone know you liked them. No, it wasn't the do-you-like-me-circle-yes-or-no note. It most certainly wasn't actually telling them that you liked them. Oh, the horror.

There was only one thing that could accurately convey your feelings for someone else. The all-powerful mixtape.

For those of us born into the era of Spotify and Apple Music, let me explain.

Back in the Stone Age, when you wanted to listen to music, you didn't simply pop open Pandora or make a Spotify list. No, you grabbed a small rectangular piece of plastic called a cassette tape. If you wanted to drop your favorite tunes into one handy-dandy place, you grabbed a blank tape, usually with "Memorex" stamped on it, and got ready to record.

Once you had your blank tape ready, you needed one other vital piece of equipment—the two-tape-deck boom box. Yeah, baby. The kind Zac Morris carries around if you stream old episodes of *Saved By the Bell* on Netflix. You slid your blank tape into one side of the deck, and the tape with your favorite song on it went into the other deck. Then came the tricky part. You had to be very careful and pay attention. There was no drag-and-drop. No fast-forwarding to the end. Nope. Once you hit Play and Record, you had to listen to the entire song. Seriously, the whole song.

You couldn't get too busy teasing your four-inch bangs or applying your blue eye shadow and miss the end of the song. If you missed hitting Pause, the beginning of the following song was on your mixtape, and you were a total amateur. Unacceptable.

Once the first song was complete, you picked a new tape with another favorite song and repeated the process until the front and back of your mixtape was complete. It took hours. Hours, people.

Then you'd roll into school the next day, walk up to that guy you liked, and hand him your mixtape. That was the most powerful way to let someone know you liked them.

Often, we have a mix tape that will play over and over in our minds. It might contain tunes like "You'll Never Be Good Enough" or "You'll Always be a Failure." We constantly replay lyrics like "How can I ever be who I'm supposed to be?" or "Maybe God made a mistake with me."

That tape plays over and over in our minds. We hear the voices of playground bullies, abusive parents, mean girls, rude cousins, gossipy students, or the ever-present harsh inner critic.

It is time to hit Stop. Time to record a new tape. Time to let a new song ring in our ears. Time to let new lyrics play in our minds.

It is time to make a new mixtape. Time to allow new songs to start playing in your mind. Drop some new tunes onto the mix tape below. Remind yourself what God says about you.

Let me get you started with a few fresh lyrics.

I have been made right (Romans 5:1).

I am called (Romans 8:30).

I am God's child (John 1:12).

I am God's workmanship (Ephesians 2:10).

I am His beloved (Jeremiah 31:3).

I am forgiven (1 Peter 2:24).

Side A

Side B

I may not feel like I am enough of a friend, enough of a student, enough of a daughter, enough of a leader. I just simply feel like I'm not enough.

But that's okay. Because God is more than enough. Through the strength and power of Jesus, I am enough too.

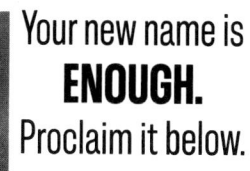
Your new name is
ENOUGH.
Proclaim it below.

MY NAME IS

Enough

8. Too Much

Recently my mom's friend Liz told her about a conversation she had with her daughter, who said, "I'm pretty sure everyone was annoyed with me."

Liz's jaw dropped as she looked at the beautiful girl telling her about the recent experience at a meeting she had attended with some other preachers' daughters. She assured her there was no way anyone would think she was annoying. After all, she was gorgeous, funny, smart, creative, and a ray of sunshine everywhere she went.

"No, I'm serious," she continued. "A lot of the girls were really standoffish with me. I think my personality was just too big for them." Liz tried to tell her the other girls were probably just shy, that she doubted anyone would think that. But her daughter was positive. She bluntly summarized, "In fact, a couple of weeks later they even unfollowed me on Instagram! I think they thought I was just too much."

A few days later, as I was mulling this conversation over in my head, I realized she wasn't the only one with a larger-than-life personality. It is possible a lot of us just might have that kind of personality too.

Have you ever felt like too much? Too loud? Too energetic? Too talented?
Too boisterous? Too strong? Too opinionated?

Fill in the blank below.

I AM TOO...

!

Michal leaned out of her window and rolled her eyes as she looked out and saw her husband dancing wildly, celebrating extravagantly, and basically acting like a fool in front of the people. And in his underwear no less. How unbecoming, she thought as her heart filled with scorn. He is just too much.

Later that day, she had a little talk with her husband, who also happened to be David the king of Israel, and told him exactly what she thought of his ridiculous display. You would think that he might have apologized for embarrassing her or maybe told her he wouldn't do something like that again. Wrong! Not only did he tell her he wasn't sorry, but he said, "Oh yes, I'll dance to God's glory—more recklessly even than this. And as far as I'm concerned ... I'll gladly look like a fool ... but among these maids you're so worried about, I'll be honored no end" (2 Samuel 6:21-22, MSG). Basically he was saying, "Oh yeah? You think that was too much? You ain't seen nothing yet! I'm getting ready to kick it up a notch!"

Clearly we can learn a thing or two from David's life.

First, some people won't understand why you do the things you do. They won't understand your personality or how you think and act. They might think you are just a little (or a lot) too much. That's okay. When King David was faced with not just any old criticism but the criticism of his own wife, he brushed it off. Instead of feeling badly about himself and his actions, he shrugged his shoulders and moved on. There may come a time when someone is critical of your big personality, and you can do the same thing. Look them square in the face and tell them you are boldly living your life for God's glory! If they choose to stick around and be a part of it, that's great, but if not, that's all right too.

David said he would gladly look like a fool in order to honor God. I think of the words that the Lord told Samuel the prophet back before he anointed David as the king: "The Lord doesn't see things the way you see them. People judge by outward appearance, but the Lord looks at the heart" (1

Samuel 16:7). What may seem foolish to others might actually be bringing glory to God. God doesn't see things the way we do. He sees past the surface and goes straight to the heart of a person.

Instead of seeing yourself as too much, recognize your uniqueness! God created you just the way you are. He loves your big, bold personality, and He will use it for His glory![9]

Set this book down.
Put your favorite dance song on.
Turn the volume up.
And dance! Go big.
Five minutes of uninhibited silliness
might be just what you need!

If you've ever felt like maybe you were just too much, you are in good company. There is a story in the New Testament about a lady who was too much in everyone else's eyes—but who Jesus said was unforgettable.

Jesus was visiting the home of one of the religious leaders when a woman interrupted the party. She came in with a huge jug of very expensive perfume, knelt down, and began to anoint Jesus's feet. She was so overwhelmed that she began to cry and washed His feet with her tears. Then she used her hair to dry them. This woman didn't have the best reputation, and the guests at the party were horrified by her behavior. I guess you could say she was a little too much for them. The Pharisees second-guessed her motives, criticized her, and had many different opinions about what she should have been doing besides her extreme display of worship.

Jesus, however, had something different to say. He defended her. First, He asked, "Why are you giving this woman a hard time?" (Matthew 26:10-13, MSG). Then He corrected them by saying, "She has just done something wonderfully significant for me." Last, He followed up with these momentous words: "You can be sure that wherever in the whole world the Message is preached, what she has just done is going to be remembered and admired."

Think about that for a moment. The Bible is full of stories about great men and women who did amazing things, but I don't recall there being anyone else who was spoken of in this way. This woman whom others thought was too much not only was recognized by Jesus for her extraordinary, extravagant act of love but will be remembered and admired all over the world until the end of time.[10]

What would you like to be remembered for?
What legacy do you want to leave?

The next time you are tempted to think of yourself as "too much," embrace who you are and be authentically you regardless of what anyone else may think. The only one you answer to is Jesus, and if you live your life in a way that uses your "too muchness" to extravagantly love Him, His admiration is all you need.

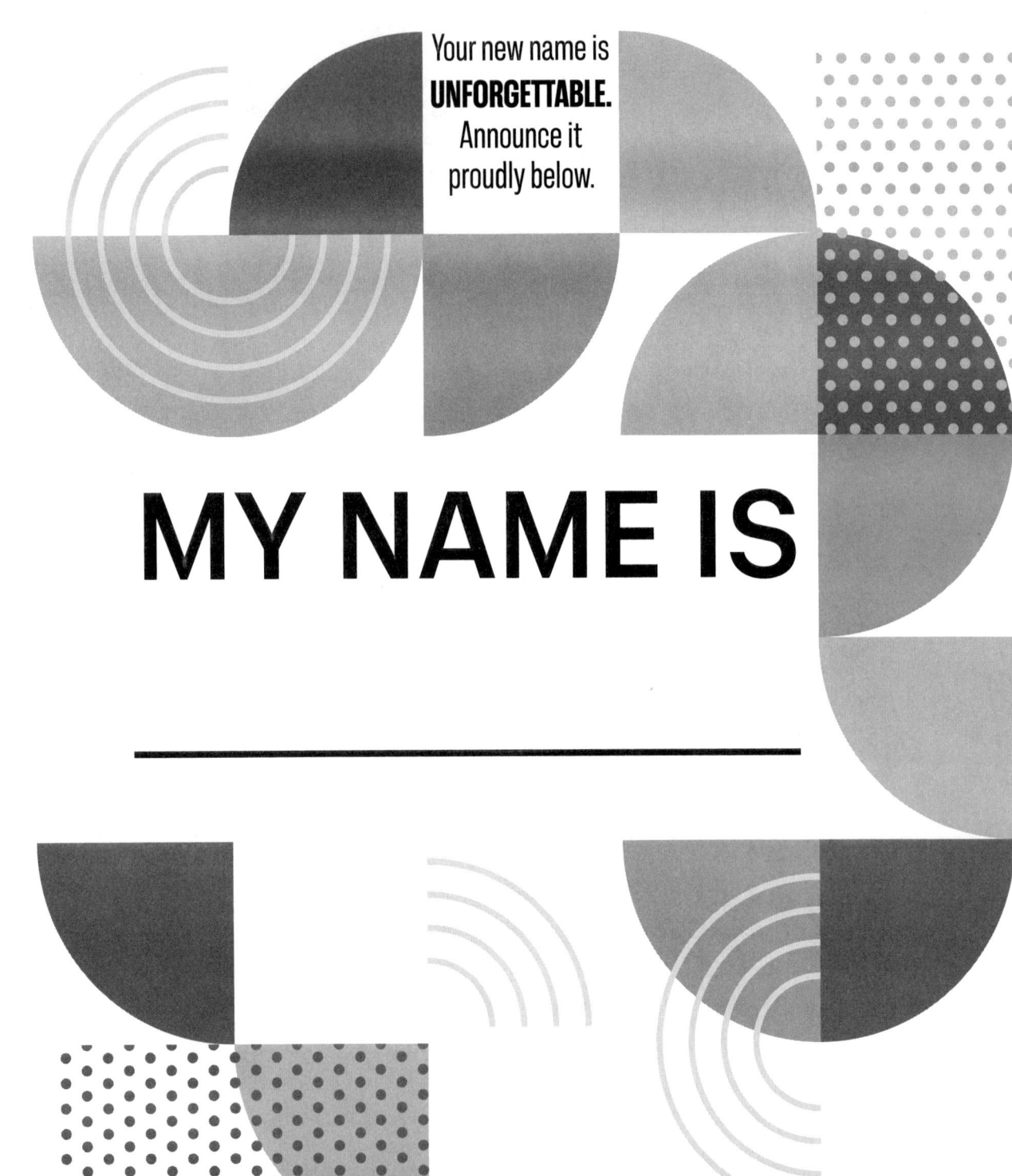

Your new name is
UNFORGETTABLE.
Announce it
proudly below.

MY NAME IS

_____

9. Rejected

A year or so ago I got the opportunity to travel to California with my school's choir. It was loads of fun, but when you share a small hotel room with six teenage girls, there are bound to be a few accidents.

I decided to look nice for a change and requested for my friend, Kira, to curl my hair. I sat letting her play hairdresser, which I soon regretted. Of course, the more Kira and I chatted, the less she paid attention to how close that curling iron was to my ear. Suddenly, I heard my ear sizzling. I jerked away as quickly as I could, but not before the blisters already started to form.

This accident left me teary eyed in the bathroom, holding ice to the burn, and surrounded by my friends who were being very "helpful" as they proceeded to Snapchat my suffering. Thanks, friends.

It certainly wasn't the first burn I've sustained; it was just the one of the painful ones I've had on my body. But there are lots of different kinds of burns. Maybe you've felt the sting of rejection. A close friend betrays you. The gossip that floats around about your family. That classmate who questions every single decision you make. The teacher who tears you down behind your back. The social media comments that sling criticism.

Burn. Burn. BURN.

Once the initial panic wore off from my curling iron accident, I ran and Googled what to do with my blistering burn. And my gosh, it seemed that the advice I found could be applied to all kinds of burns, including the burns of rejection.

PRAYER IS OFTEN OUR LAST LINE OF DEFENSE, WHEN IT SHOULD BE  OUR FIRST.

—Brandi Wilson

HOW TO TREAT A MINOR BURN AT HOME

STEP 1:

First hold the burn under cold running water for ten to fifteen minutes. If cold running water is not available, immerse the burn in cold water or cover it with cold compresses.

Our first step when treating a burn is to immediately turn to the Living Water. Not for a few drops. Not a little sprinkle. But a full immersion in the restoration offered by the Living Water. It may be ten to fifteen minutes or ten to fifteen days, but our first step should be total immersion in Jesus. We need to let Jesus wash over us—cooling, cleansing, calming.

For the next five or ten minutes, hit Pause. Sit with Jesus.

Need a place to start? Meditate on who Jesus says He is:

The Bread of Life. "I am the bread of life. Whoever comes to me will never go hungry, and whoever believes in me will never be thirsty" (John 6:35, NIV).

The Light of the World. "I am the light of the world. Whoever follows me will never walk in darkness, but will have the light of life" (John 8:12, NIV).

The Gate. "I am the gate; whoever enters through me will be saved. They will come in and go out, and find pasture" (John 10:9, NIV).

The Good Shepherd. "I am the good shepherd. The good shepherd lays down his life for the sheep" (John 10:11, NIV).

The Resurrection and the Life. "I am the resurrection and the life. The one who believes in me will live, even though they die; and whoever lives by believing in me will never die" (John 11:25-26, NIV).

The Way. The Truth. The Life. "I am the way and the truth and the life. No one comes to the Father except through me" (John 14:6, NIV).

The Vine. "I am the vine; you are the branches. If you remain in me and I in you, you will bear much fruit; apart from me you can do nothing" (John 15:5, NIV).

HOW TO TREAT A MINOR BURN AT HOME

STEP 2:
Do not apply butter to the burn. Butter will trap heat in the damaged tissues, which can potentially cause more damage and increase your chance of developing an infection.

Do not do anything that could trap the heat—bitterness, anger, hurt—in your burn. The damage caused by allowing that hurt to be trapped inside can be more damaging than the burn itself. Don't build walls and barriers around your heart. Don't isolate yourself in silence and fear. Don't stuff your emotions, refusing to deal with them honestly. Stay away from the butter.

- -

Write the most hurtful things people have said about you, your friends, your family. Get it out.

Now tear this page out and burn it. That's right, light it on fire. Scorch these hurtful words. Reduce them to ashes. Absolutely decimate them. Remember, God is in the business of bringing beauty from ashes. Don't allow these burns to stay inside any longer.

MATURING

MEANS REALIZING HOW MANY THINGS

DON'T NECESSARILY REQUIRE

YOUR COMMENT.

—Kimberly Scott

HOW TO TREAT A MINOR BURN AT HOME

STEP 3:

Once the burn has cooled via cold water or compress exposure, apply lotion to the area. Lotion may soothe any discomfort that you feel and will also prevent dryness.

One of the best healing balms is gratitude. When we are burned, we can take our focus off our injuries and instead fix our gaze on the many things we can be thankful for.

Psalm 103 is a verbal explosion of thankfulness for all that the Lord has done for us. Take a few minutes to pray through these personalized verses. Highlight or circle all of the things we can be thankful for.

Let all that I am praise You, Lord;
   with my whole heart, I will praise Your holy name.
Let all that I am praise You, Lord;
   may I never forget the good things You have done for me.
You forgive all my sins
   and heal all my diseases.
You redeem me from death
   and crown me with love and tender mercies.
You fill my life with good things.
   My youth is renewed like the eagle's!
Lord, You give righteousness
   and justice to all who are treated unfairly.
You, Lord, are compassionate and merciful,
   slow to get angry and filled with unfailing love.
You will not constantly accuse me,
   nor remain angry forever.

You do not punish me for all my sins;
   You do not deal harshly with me, as I deserve.
For Your unfailing love toward those who fear You
   is as great as the height of the heavens above the earth.
You have removed my sins as far from me
   as the east is from the west.
Lord, You are like a father to Your children,
   tender and compassionate to those who fear You.

King Nebuchadnezzar acted like a fool by having a ninety-foot-tall statue built in his honor. It was in gold, people. GOLD. The plan was, people all over would bow down to the statue and worship it every time they heard the musical instruments play. Almost everyone did ... except three Jewish men.

> Some of the astrologers went to the king and informed on the Jews. They said to King Nebuchadnezzar, "Long live the king! You issued a decree requiring all the people to bow down and worship the gold statue when they hear the sound of the horn, flute, zither, lyre, harp, pipes, and other musical instruments. That decree also states that those who refuse to obey must be thrown into a blazing furnace. But there are some Jews—Shadrach, Meshach, and Abednego—whom you have put in charge of the province of Babylon. They pay no attention to you, Your Majesty. They refuse to serve your gods and do not worship the gold statue you have set up." (Daniel 3:8-12)

The king, who had a bit of a temper problem, was infuriated! He flew into a rage and dragged Shadrach, Meshach, and Abednego in to question them and extend one last opportunity to worship his statue right then and there.

> Shadrach, Meshach, and Abednego replied, "O Nebuchadnezzar, we do not need to defend ourselves before you. If we are thrown into the blazing furnace, the God whom we serve is able to save us. He will rescue us from your power, Your Majesty. But even if he doesn't, we want to make it clear to you, Your Majesty, that we will never serve your gods or worship the gold statue you have set up." (verses 16-18)

Oh no they didn't. Someone was going down for that reply even though it was crazy bold. King Nebuchadnezzar was so mad his face became distorted with rage. Yikes. He was so furious he had those three young men thrown into a fiery furnace. Not just a regular ol' fiery furnace. No.

A furnace that was heated seven times hotter!

With their hands bound, they were tossed into the fire—a fire so hot it consumed the guards when they threw Shadrach, Meshach, and Abednego in. While some might think God did not come through on His end of the deal, He so did. Hold, please.

When the king looked into the furnace, he saw four men walking around in there. Excuse me? Yes, there were four men walking around in the furnace, and one of them looked like a god!

King Nebuchadnezzar snuck as close to the furnace door as he could and yelled, "Shadrach, Meshach, and Abednego, servants of the Most High God, come out!" (verse 26).

When they came out of the furnace, there wasn't a burn mark on their clothes. Officials quickly surrounded them and "saw that the fire had not touched them. Not a hair on their heads was singed, and their clothing was not scorched. They didn't even smell of smoke!" (verse 27).

They didn't even smell like smoke. Have you ever sat by a fire while roasting marshmallows and come back inside reeking of smoke? And that's just sitting by a fire. These boys were in the fire, and they did not smell like smoke.[11]

We all get burned in life. Unfortunately, there is no way to stay completely burn and rejection free. But we can choose to not go through the rest of our lives smelling like smoke from the ones who burned us. They don't deserve that much impact. And it is a poor representation of our Savior if everywhere we go we leave a trail of smoke behind from what others have done.

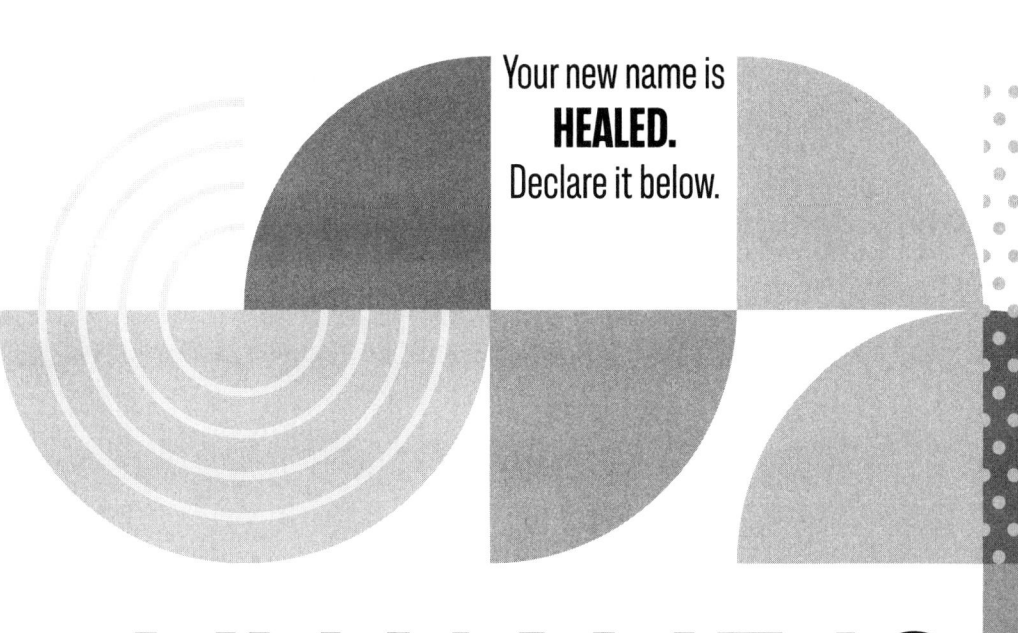

Your new name is
HEALED.
Declare it below.

MY NAME IS

HEALED

10. Bitter

Every Christmas I ask my parents for a new phone. All my friends would receive the newest and coolest iPhone, and I always wanted to be right up there with them. When my mom told me she was giving me a new phone, I was so excited! I knew, holding my old phone, that the latest and greatest was coming out, and I couldn't wait to be up to date in the tech world. Then my mom passed down her old phone and proceeded to buy herself the newest model of the iPhone. At first, I was super excited even though it wasn't the most recent phone, but then I started to see my friends' phones, and I circled back to where I had begun - wanting the new phone.

While I was very grateful, I also couldn't help be a little bit bitter, especially now that my phone turns off at any exposure to extreme cold/hot weather, which is a problem when you live in a place that hits 115 degrees in the summer. Now, it can't take pictures anymore, so the bitterness comes in full-force when my mom busts out her phone proceeding to take all her pictures in portrait mode. Dang. Rude.

I've heard it said that complaining is calling into question the provision, sovereignty, and rule of God in my life and saying it isn't good enough for me. Complaining is looking at God and saying everything He's provided isn't good enough for me.

If we aren't careful, bitterness can easily creep into our lives so easily. We look around our schools and we think: God, You surrounded me here to these crazy, hurting people. And this just isn't good enough for me.

Or maybe you don't love what God has you doing right now and think: I could have more influence and do more for the Lord. This just isn't good enough for me.

We have a tendency to take that complaining spirit, turn it back on God, and say His provision isn't good enough for us.

What's your "cell phone"?
What bitterness are you carrying around with you?

We aren't the only ones who can fall easily into the trap of complaining and bitterness. In Numbers 11:1 we read, "Soon the people began to complain to the Lord."

We know the story of the Israelites as they leave behind their lives of slavery in Egypt. They have miraculously walked on dry land as God parted the Red Sea. God has led them by a pillar of fire and a cloud of smoke. Can you even imagine? Amazing!

But "the people began to complain to the Lord."

And the Lord said: "Oh, you poor babies. Here is a Band-aid and a lollipop, and we're going to make it all better!"

No! That's not what the Bible says at all.

It says, "The Lord's anger blazed against them." I don't know about you, but I haven't always understood how seriously the Lord takes that complaining spirit.

"The Lord's anger burned against them, and he sent a fire to rage among them." Was that because they were experiencing hardships and troubles? No. It was because in those hardships and troubles they had an attitude of complaining. The Lord was angry, absolutely furious. In the midst of blessing after blessing, the Israelites were bitter. They complained because, at the core, they felt the provision of God simply wasn't good enough for them.

As Numbers 11 wraps up, the Bible says God's "anger blazed out against the people. He hit them with a terrible plague. They ended up calling the place Kibroth Hattaavah (Graves-of-the-Craving)" (verse 34, MSG).

Graves of craving. What a powerful image! Are we building for ourselves graves of craving, or are we living lives of gratitude?

Are you building graves of craving?
> *If I only had more friends.*
> *If I only had more money.*
> *If I only had more talent.*
> *If I only had more Instagram followers.*
> *If I only had more resources.*
> *If I only had more, more, more.*

What graves of craving have you been building?
Write them on the earth below the headstones.

Let's not build ourselves graves of craving. Instead, let's live lives of gratitude.

Not too long ago, my parents hopped on a plane bound for Hawaii, where they were doing a wedding for friends. For the first hour everything went splendidly. My mom settled in to watch the rom com downloaded to her computer when suddenly their flight attendant came over the speaker with this announcement: "We're having a little problem with one of our passengers. Please stay in your seats. Mahalo."

Mahalo is a lovely little Hawaiian word expressing thanks and gratitude. It made my parents feel a little warm and cozy, like everything was under control and fine. They got out the snack they'd picked up at the airport Starbucks, hit Play on their movie, and readied themselves for their over-ocean flight.

Just about the time my film was getting good, another announcement was made: "Unfortunately, we are going to need to turn the plane around and head back to Los Angeles. Please remain in your seats. Mahalo."

Wait. What?!

As they landed at LAX, announcement number three hit the speakers: "Law enforcement will be boarding the plane. Please do not get up. We will be back on our way as soon as possible. Mahalo."

And board they did. Two police officers boarded the plane to remove a man who had pitched a fit over not wanting to pay $12 for a blanket. Yep. Their flight was rerouted over a blanket. A $12 blanket. If they had known, my parents would have given the guy twelve bucks. Instead he told the flight attendant he was going to "take her out behind the woodshed." When you threaten a flight attendant, no matter how stupidly, you get hauled off the plane by law enforcement.

Let me now encapsulate the following five—yes, five—hours at LAX by sharing the airline announcements.

"You may now move about the plane while we finish paperwork to get us on our way again. Mahalo."

"We are sorry we will no longer be able to serve food on this flight. It is against the health code to reheat the food. So there will be nothing to eat on your flight. Mahalo."

"Unfortunately our pilot has now timed out, and we are going to need to get another crew. Mahalo."

"We are now going to take you off the plane and back to the LAX airport. Unfortunately we are in a remote lot, so you will need to ride shuttle buses to the main terminal. Mahalo."

"As you enter the gate, make sure to take a voucher for a free lunch at the airport. Mahalo."

"We hope you are enjoying your free lunch. It will be a couple of more hours until we have a new flight crew. Mahalo."

"We hope you have had time to eat the free lunch we've provided you. We have a flight crew en route, but it will be a while. Mahalo."

"We are now going to need to move you all to another gate. We hope you enjoyed your free lunch. Mahalo."

"We will now be reboarding our flight. Unfortunately, we will be so late that any connecting flight will need to be rebooked for tomorrow. Mahalo."

My parents decided a couple of things as they finally headed back toward Hawaii. First, if anyone complained about blankets, they were going to take them behind the woodshed. They just wouldn't tell them until the plane landed. Second, no matter how bad the news you are delivering, if you sweetly say the word "mahalo" at the end, apparently everything will be okay.

Is that truly the power of a thank-you? Maybe not, but it really, really helps.

Turn back to the graves of craving. For every grave of craving that has bitterness and complaint buried below, write something you are thankful for on the headstone crosses. Let's move our focus above our grievances and instead remind ourselves of all we have to be thankful for.

Our favorite prescription to fight bitterness is from Ella, a missionary to the Pygmies in Africa for fifty-two years.[12] The italics are from Ella; the rest are our thoughts:

1. *Never allow yourself to complain about anything—not even the weather.* Not the lack of help. Not the lack of money. Not the lack of a home. Not the classmate who drives you crazy. Not the little brother who is creating trouble. Not the person who is gossiping. Not the decision you would have made differently. Not the busyness of your calendar. Nothing— nothing at all.

2. *Never picture yourself in any other circumstances or someplace else.* Remember that the grass isn't always greener someplace else. Maybe, as the great theologian Sebastian the crab sings to Ariel, although it may seem "the seaweed is always greener in somebody else's lake," that doesn't make it a more beautiful green than the seaweed in your own lake. Focus on the blessings in front of you instead of imagining how much better it would be elsewhere.

3. *Never compare your lot with another's.*

Leave behind thoughts like these:
> *If I had as much money as this person…*
> *If I were as popular as this person…*
> *If only I could have a more exciting life…*
> *…then things would be easier/better/more filling/more enjoyable.*

Those thoughts are sure-fired ways to grow in bitterness.

4. *Never allow yourself to wish this or that had been otherwise.*

We can live in "if only" and be haunted by things that we cannot change, or we can trust the past to God, knowing He will work all things for good for those who love Christ.

5. Never dwell on tomorrow—remember that tomorrow is God's, not ours.

Obviously we need to dream big and plan for tomorrow, but we cannot let those dreams be choked by worry. We believe God holds our tomorrows, but sometimes it is so hard to pry our fingers off and let Him carry them.

Let's commit ourselves to lives of gratitude. Mahalo.

Your new name is **GRATEFUL.** Shout it out below.

MY NAME IS

_____

Group Discussion Questions

1. Share three things that are special about you, the things that help you bloom.

2. If you were to pop open your music library to make a mixtape today, what is one song that would have to be on it? What mixtape of negative chatter plays over and over in your mind?

3. Fill in the blank: I am too _____. What makes you feel that way?

4. What burns of rejection have you sustained? What steps can you take to keep from smelling like smoke?

5. List one grave of craving you've built. What is something you can be thankful for to help you raise your focus above the bitterness?

Session 3

11. Depressed

Maybe it is the move. The packing up. The leaving the house you loved. The distance from friends.

Maybe it is the overwhelming fear. The anxiety that we can't measure up. The stress that we won't be able to meet expectations.

Maybe it is not liking what we see in the mirror. The insecurity. The self-loathing. The wishing we looked a different way.

Maybe it is a funk. Maybe it is all of that combined. Whatever the cause, depression and discouragement can take hold of us.

When we are in a dark place in our lives. We can simply feel like the lights have gone out. No matter how much we grope around in the dark searching for the light switch, we simply can't find it. We desperately want our lives to be flooded with light again; we just can't figure out how to access that light.

When you feel surrounded by darkness, remember all God did in the light. He can do it again, even though it may feel dark right now. Write the things God did during the light on the bulbs below.

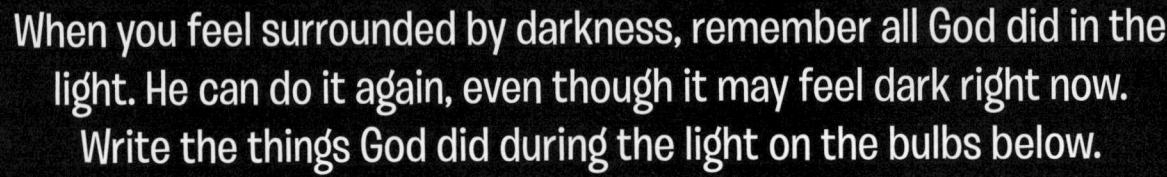

Everyone has at least one thing they refuse to let go. Whether it be your favorite skinny jeans that don't seem to fit anymore, that one shirt that is comfy yet devastated by mystery stains, or that baby blanket that has seen better days.

I'm not afraid to admit that I have a few things I won't let go. I tend to hang onto everything. My mom has called me a "hoarder" many times. I just can't seem to get rid of my treasures. I still refuse to get rid of a single one of my thirty-two snow globes even though they collect dust in the back of my closet. I can't part ways with the stuffed animals my preschool friends gifted me although I can't remember the names of those kids who gave them to me any more. And I'm not about to donate any of my concert tees, not even that R-5 shirt from my Disney days.

I have a white-knuckled, iron-fisted death grip on my stuff.

So I hang on.

I wish that I held on to more things in my life with that kind of tenacity. But I hear ugly gossip going around about my family, and I let go of my joy. Criticism starts to flow our direction, and I loosen my grip on peace.

Expectations rise … loneliness chokes … anxiety appears …

And I release confidence … security … my sense of purpose …

There is one thing, though, that it is vital that we hold on to when depression and discouragement are haunting us. We have to keep a grip on hope.

> I'll never forget the trouble, the utter lostness,
>   the taste of ashes, the poison I've swallowed.

I remember it all—oh, how well I remember—
  the feeling of hitting the bottom.
But there's one other thing I remember,
  and remembering, I keep a grip on hope.

(Lamentations 3:19-21, MSG)

We've heard discouragement described as the melting away of our joy. When our joy seems to be in a puddle at our feet, we feel utterly lost. The taste in our mouths is not sweet happiness but instead the taste of ashes and poison. We know what it feels like to hit the bottom. That's precisely when we need to keep a grip on hope.

This section of Scripture is found smack dab in the middle of the book of Lamentations. All around it is woe, sadness, hurt, and lament. What rises up out of the center is the hope of Jesus Christ. When our lives are surrounded by woe, sadness, hurt, and lament, the hope of Jesus rises up.

So let us hold tightly—with a white-knuckled, iron-fisted death grip—on hope because our loving God is faithful.

God's loyal love couldn't have run out,
  his merciful love couldn't have dried up.
They're created new every morning.
  How great your faithfulness!
I'm sticking with God (I say it over and over).
  He's all I've got left. (verses 22-24, MSG)

Together, let's tighten our grasp, hang on, and cling to the hope of Jesus. He is all we have left.

NOW I AM DEEPLY DISCOURAGED,
BUT I WILL **REMEMBER** YOU.

EACH DAY THE LORD POURS HIS
UNFAILING LOVE
UPON ME,

AND THROUGH
EACH NIGHT

I SING
HIS
SONGS

PRAYING TO GOD
WHO GIVES ME **LIFE.**

—Psalm 42:6, 8

4:30 a.m., May 23, 2013.

A small tugboat off the coast of Nigeria carrying twelve crew members, including cook Harrison Odjegba Okene, capsized and sank to the bottom of the Atlantic.

As the boat sank, Okene managed to find an air bubble and a bottle of Coke for sustenance. Temperatures dropped to freezing, and he recited the psalm his wife texted him before bedtime:

> Save me, O God, by your name. ...
> The Lord is the one who sustains me. (Psalm 54:1, 4, NIV)

The hours crept by. Okene became frightened as he heard the sounds of sharks or barracudas swimming around the boat, eating, and "fighting over something big." Harrison was freezing and quickly running out of air.[13]

Worst-case scenario. But, unbelievably, the "worst" wasn't the worst.

Sixty hours after the sinking of the ship, divers were attempting to recover the bodies of the crew. One diver spied a hand in the murky water. Assuming he'd found another corpse, the diver reached out to grab the hand ... and the hand grabbed back! Can you even imagine?!

After being entombed on the ocean floor for almost three days, Harrison Okene had survived. He had not been left alone.

You may feel like you are drowning in despair, barely breathing, only just surviving. You may feel like you are trapped in the "worst." Be comforted:

> The "worst" is never the worst.
> Why? Because the Master won't ever
> walk out and fail to return.

If He works severely, he also works tenderly.
His stockpiles of loyal love are immense.

(Lamentations 3:30-32, MSG)

You are not alone in your "worst." God is, in fact, reaching through the murky waters of your life and taking hold of your hand. He has promised His presence even in the middle of your discouragement, in the midst of your despair, and at the midpoint of your depression.

Why? Because "His stockpiles of loyal love are immense." We love that. What a beautiful picture of the Lord's love. His loyal love. The stockpiles of His love for you are so immense that He will never walk out on you. He is with you. He loves you. Hope in that today.

....

....

....

....

....

....

....

....

....

....

....

....

....

....

....

Now, take a big, black sharpie, and write "**God**" in giant letters on top of your "worst." The worst is never the worst because He is with you in the midst of your pain.

Your new name is
HOPE.
Proudly claim it
below.

MY NAME IS

_____

12. Empty

My brother, Ethan, came roaring into this world at eight pounds, ten ounces, and a whopping two weeks early, meaning God saved my mom from a ten-and-a-half-pound baby. When Ethan was an infant, he wore my parents out. He woke up every two hours for the first few months so he could eat, eat, eat. They were absolutely exhausted.

When we would visit the pediatrician, they would take all of his measurements, raise their eyebrows, and jot down on his growth chart: 99 percent with an up arrow. An up arrow, people. Which means he was taller than more than 99 percent of the kids his age.

My baby brother, my teeny-tiny buddy, is now a fourteen-year-old, six-foot-one-inch gentle giant. He wears Shaquille O'Neal–looking 12.5 double wide men's shoes that we have to special-order. He hands down clothes to our dad. In order to discipline him eyeball to eyeball, Mom has to stand on the bottom step of our stairs while he stands on the floor.

In order to fuel that kind of growth, he requires lots and lots of food. Ethan is a bottomless pit. There is not enough tortellini in the world to fill that empty stomach. As he says, "I've only been full, like, five times in my whole life." That's why my mom taught him to cook for himself.

Isn't this just like life? We fill up ... and are vacant in no time. We nourish ourselves ... and quickly feel depleted. We take in ... only to be emptied out.

We pour into others, serve our families, help our friends, better our communities, and support our co-workers.

And we feel flat-out empty.

How full or empty are you right now? Draw in the arrow to indicate how much gas you have in the tank.

What makes you feel empty?

....

....

....

....

....

....

Oh boy, have we ever felt empty. It might be after a long week of checking off to-dos on an overstuffed calendar. The emptiness might come after a period of being away from home and instead frequenting sports practices or musical rehearsals. It may show up after the bickering has ratcheted up among your siblings, and you can only find a moment of peace by locking yourself in the bathroom. We may feel empty after a day of climbing the Mount Everest of homework. I'm convinced there is nothing more draining than never-ending study guides. Nothing.

We don't know what drains you. Maybe it isn't those things at all. No matter what, we can all relate to feeling empty.

The prophet Elijah follows God's direction and rolls into the village of Zarephath during an extreme drought. As he nears the gate, he sees a widow gathering sticks to build one last cooking fire. He calls out, requesting a cup of water, and as she turns to get him one, Elijah adds: "Oh hey! Grab me a piece of bread while you're at it."

Seriously?!

She replies, "I swear by the Lord your God that I don't have a single piece of bread in the house. And I have only a handful of flour left in the jar and a little cooking oil in the bottom of the jug. I was just gathering a few sticks to cook this last meal, and then my son and I will die" (1 Kings 17:12).

That's what I call running on empty. The fewest ingredients for a single last meal. That's it. Nothing left. Completely depleted.

Then Elijah continues, "Don't be afraid! Go ahead and do just what you've said, but make a little bread for me first. Then use what's left to prepare a meal for yourself and your son. For this is what the Lord, the God of Israel, says: There will always be flour and olive oil left in your containers until the time when the Lord sends rain and the crops grow again!" (verses 13-14).

The widow offered the little bit she had, and they ate. And ate. And ate. There was always enough left in her containers, just as God promised. The jars never became empty. She always had enough.

Wouldn't it be incredible if our jars never became empty? Maybe if we connect with the Lord and lean in to His promises, we can avoid that emptiness.

What fills you up? Circle below.

COOKING

READING

PRAYER

TIME WITH
FRIENDS

ALONE
TIME

JOURNALING

BUBBLE
BATH

WORSHIP
MUSIC

SERVING

NATURE

HOBBIES

OTHERS

....

....

....

....

The friends need help understanding the homework. The family needs time together. The room needs to be cleaned. The bestie needs a listening ear. The parents need an extra hand around the house. The church needs volunteers for the event this weekend. The neighbor needs a babysitter. There simply isn't time in the day to take care of ourselves. How could we be selfish when surrounded by such great need?

Stop. Hold it right there for a second.

Self-care is not selfish. Nope, it's surely not.

Making the time to ensure we aren't running on empty isn't just important; it is vital if we want to be healthy people with healthy families, healthy friendships, a healthy school life, and a healthy life of faith.

Self-care starts with learning what helps us feel strong, what makes us feel connected to God.

For you, worship music may be the perfect thing to fill you up. Just one song connects with your heart and centers you on Jesus. Stress and tension fade into the background. The music calms your spirit so you can "be still" and rest in His presence.

Or being out in creation might do the trick. You love being outside on a hike with your family taking in the uniqueness of nature. A good run on a tree-filled trail or a long trek on a bike may replenish you like nothing else. Standing on a dock or in a stream with a fishing pole in hand breathes life into you.

Another way you may stuff your soul with goodness is through serving. You love jumping in and helping where you see a need. Your heart is full after you've served God to the best of your ability. You find yourself experiencing God when you take care of those who can't take care of themselves.

A friend night out might be a gift. You soak up laughing and chatting like a sponge. Being soaked in community fills you up. You talk about faith or family, miracles or movies, needs or novels. Every conversation is good and life-giving.

Or maybe quiet is where it's at for you. Sweet serenity. No talking. No people. Just glorious alone time. Silence is golden. Time alone with your thoughts and time alone with God rejuvenates.

Maybe you're filled up by:

Playing video games	Bingeing Netflix
Getting a pedicure	Whipping up some brownies
Reading by the fire	A fun night out with friends
Writing in a journal	Soaking in a bubble bath
Crafting	Diving into a Bible study
Working out	

It's so important to know how you get refilled and what draws you closer to Jesus. And once you hone in on how you are filled, you can make it a priority to carve out some self-care time on your calendar. Because, remember, self-care isn't selfish. Self-care makes us better friends, students, children, siblings and people of faith.

Jot down opportunities for self-care this week.

If you don't schedule it, it won't happen.

SUNDAY	MONDAY	TUESDAY

WEDNESDAY	THURSDAY	FRIDAY	SATURDAY

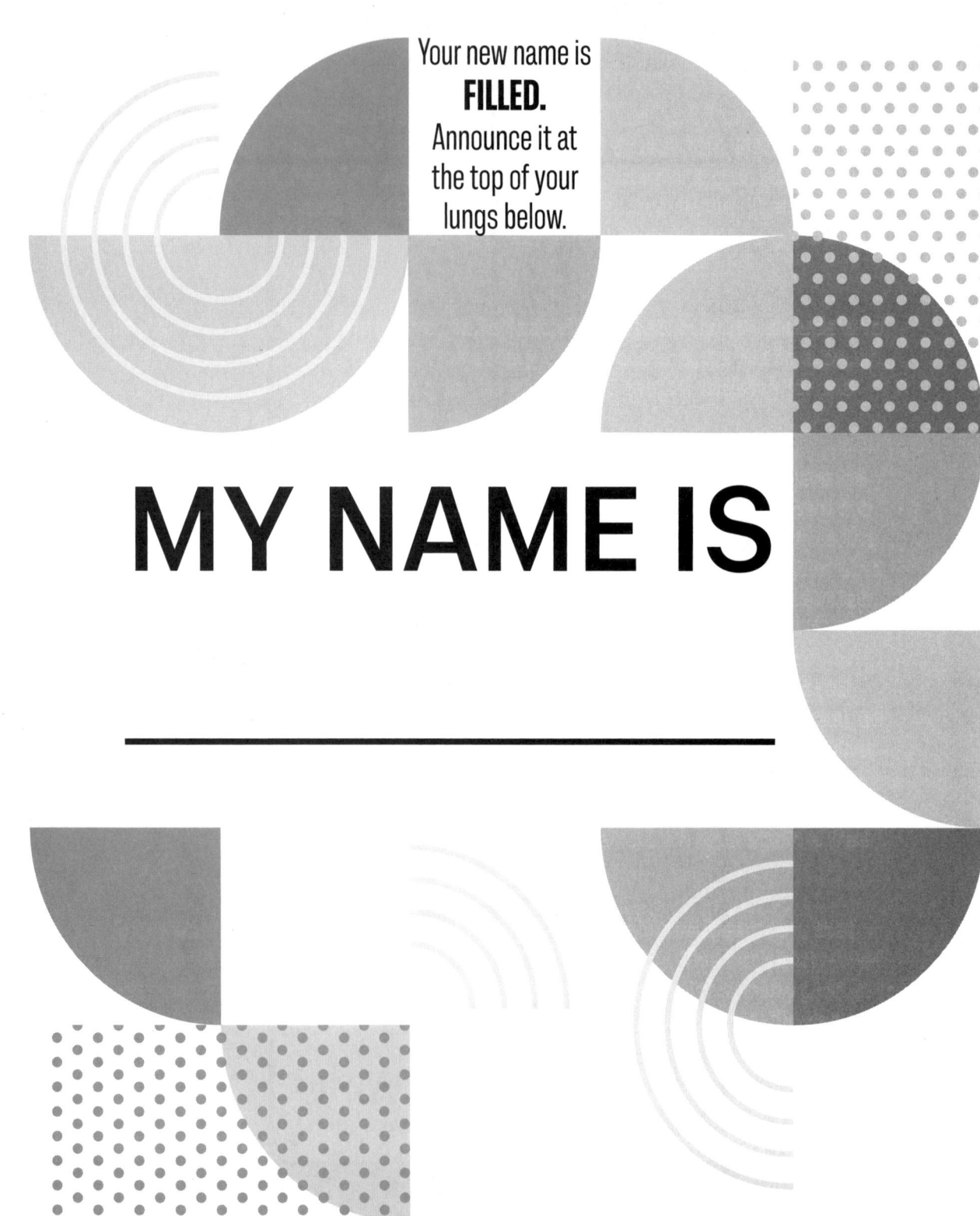

Your new name is
FILLED.
Announce it at
the top of your
lungs below.

MY NAME IS

_____

13. Homeless

Half-way through my 5th grade year, I was excited to be launching into Middle School soon. I had great friends, and I knew where I was headed. I was destined to become a Miller Mustang. That is, until, my parents let me know that they wanted to make a change in my Jr. High plans.

I would have to say goodbye to my friends. Goodbye to my neighborhood school. Goodbye to what seemed a safe and secure future.

When my class was scheduled to tour the Middle School all my friends would be going to, my mom kept me home and said, "Don't worry, babe. You're going to go to a wonderful school. Somewhere. We just don't know where, yet."

Um. Thank you? Not reassuring.

I'm not the only person who has been told to start packing because God was leading them to a mystery place. In Genesis 12 that's exactly what happened to Sarai. Her husband, Abram, had gotten a word from God, and now her whole world was about to be disrupted. She would leave her parents, siblings, and friends to wander aimlessly until Abram got his next set of instructions from up above.

A myriad of thoughts must have bombarded Sarai. Maybe she thought:
Listen, buddy, I didn't hear anything from God. Are you sure about this?
This isn't fair. Why do I have to leave my nice life behind and head out to the middle of a desert?
I'm not going to be able to talk to my mom every day?
So you have a dream, and I have to suffer now?
And we are going ... where?
Great, now I'm going to be homeless.

I think there might have been a few raging arguments around my tent before I dutifully packed my stuff and jumped on a camel to trot after my husband into the desert on our quest to fulfill the call of God on his life.

Draw your home. It might be the home you grew up in, the one you live in now, or one in between.

Draw the place that feels like home to you.

What is it that makes this place feel like home?

Home Sweet Home

We are naturally wired to desire safety and stability in our homes, to thrive when we feel secure. Alternately, when we don't feel that security, it can leave us feeling unstable and like our whole world has been shaken. It is possible to find stability even in the midst of uncertain circumstances.

Look past the pain of the moment and focus your gaze on the promises of God. When God spoke to Abram and told him to pack up and leave his home, He also gave him a few promises that would come to fulfillment on the other side of his obedience. "I will make you into a great nation. I will bless you and make you famous, and you will be a blessing to others. … All the families on earth will be blessed through you" (Genesis 12:2-3).

In those times when Sarai might have been tempted to sulk, grumble, complain, or be fearful about her situation, she could think back to the reason behind the move. God promised to bless not only her family but all the families of the earth through them. There was an end result that far outweighed how uncomfortable she might have been in the beginning.

Throughout Scripture, God makes a few promises to us, His followers, as well. Here are just a few:

> He promises to never leave us
> (Deuteronomy 31:6).
>
> He promises to give us a new heart and a new spirit
> (Ezekiel 36:26).
>
> He promises to guide us along the best pathway for our lives
> (Psalm 32:8).
>
> He promises peace when we trust Him and fix our thoughts on Him
> (Isaiah 26:3).

When we are tempted to drop our heads and sulk, grumble, complain, or be consumed by fear about our situation, we can think back on the promises of God. We can find security and stability in the Lord's promises because they are true and trustworthy. In fact, 2 Corinthians 1:20 declares, "All of God's promises have been fulfilled in Christ with a resounding 'Yes!'"

We place our trust in the Lord, not in our fickle feelings. God's ways are not ours, that's for sure! When we learn to trust Him, even when it doesn't make sense, our faith grows.

Remember the rest of Sarai's story: she gained a new name, Sarah, and had a baby even though she was far too old. The impossible became possible. Hebrews 11:11 tells us, "It was by faith that even Sarah was able to have a child, though she was barren and was too old. She believed that God would keep his promise." Who knows? Maybe because Sarai learned to trust God in her season of homelessness, she was able to trust Him to do the impossible in her life at a later time.

We can learn from her example and believe that God will keep His promises in our lives. Even if our feelings aren't quite ready to trust, we can trust anyway knowing that He will be faithful. When we follow Him in faith, He is with us even in the midst of our homelessness.[14]

Which is your favorite promise on the previous pages?

Look up the verse, and write it below. Jot it down. Commit it to memory. Don't turn the page until it's been permanently etched in your heart and mind.

The children of Israel at the time of the Babylonian exile truly experienced homelessness. They were forced out of their homes and taken into captivity by a neighboring country. Forced to leave everything they knew, they essentially started over in a place where they were strangers and unwanted for more than seventy years.

While you might not have experienced the trauma of being forced out of your home and placed in exile in a foreign country, you might understand the feeling of being put in a position where you have to let go of what is familiar and step into the unknown. The Bible shows us how God instructed the people of Israel to respond to their time of feeling homeless and gives us insight we can apply to our lives.

> This is what the Lord of Heaven's Armies, the God of Israel, says to all the captives he has exiled to Babylon from Jerusalem: "Build homes, and plan to stay. Plant gardens, and eat the food they produce. Marry and have children. Then find spouses for them so that you may have many grandchildren. Multiply! Do not dwindle away! And work for the peace and prosperity of the city where I sent you into exile. Pray to the Lord for it, for its welfare will determine your welfare." (Jeremiah 29:4-7)

Build homes, and plan to stay. Plant gardens, and eat the food they produce. Put down roots in the place where God has you planted. Focusing on where you are, rather than where you were, allows you to put down roots and find stability instead of longing to be in your old location.

Marry and have children. Then find spouses for them so that you may have many grandchildren. Multiply! Do not dwindle away! Plan to be here long term. Looking to the future gives you the chance to build excitement about the legacy you can leave instead of pining for the past.

Work for the peace and prosperity of the city where I sent you into exile.

Embrace the community to which you've been sent. Do what you can to make your location the best it can be. Find a need that you can fulfill in your city or school. Ask yourself, What can I do to make this place more peaceful or more prosperous? Then take steps to do it.

Pray to the Lord for it, for its welfare will determine your welfare. This a big one. If you are in a place where you feel homeless, without a true sense of belonging, We ask you: How much time are you spending in prayer for your new city or new school? God said the welfare of the place would determine the welfare of the people, so praying for the new place is actually praying for yourself and your family too. When we pray, God can soften our hearts and bind them to new towns, communities, people, and churches. Pray that God would give you a love for your new place and watch Him change your heart to see it as a place you can truly call home.[15]

Take a few minutes to pray for your city, school and church.
Write your prayer below.

YOU GO WHERE YOU'RE SENT.

YOU STAY WHERE YOU'RE PUT.

AND YOU GIVE WHAT YOU'VE GOT *until you're done.*

—Jill Briscoe

"Consider the lilies of the field, how they grow" (Matthew 6:28, ESV).

God plants the dainty flowers in the field and the giant oak trees in the forest. He plants the tall grass on the prairie and the palm tree on the beach. And each of those creations blooms and grows and praises Him right where He has planted them. They know their Father made them for a specific purpose. He cares for them and knows what is best. He is God, and they trust Him.

That's how we should live the life God has given us. Rest in the fact that God has made you and given you a specific purpose. He cares for you and has planted you right where you are for a reason. He is God, the Author of your story. So whether you're a giant oak in a mighty forest or you're a tiny daisy standing alone, stop looking over the fence at someone else's grass.

Bloom where you've been planted!

Your new name is
AT HOME.
Proclaim it below.

MY NAME IS

At Home

14. Overlooked

Earlier this year, I invited both my parents to attend my school's chapel service because I was preforming a duet. I was super nervous but also excited to have my parents in attendance to support me. After I finished my performance and the service was over, I fought against the crowds of the student body to go say hi to my mom and dad.

When I finally got to them, I only said a couple words before this kid, Blake, interrupted us. He said hello to my dad, declaring how much he liked our church and my dad's messages. My dad asked him a few questions about school before Blake finally walked off to get back to class.

After pseudo-patiently standing there, I realized two things. First, this kid totally stole my spotlight. Dude, my parents were there to see me, not chat it up with you. Secondly, that kid had sat next to me in Spanish since the very beginning of the school year, and he hadn't said two words to me.

Seriously?! Fantastic. It's safe to say, I was a bit peeved and quite annoyed. I obviously make a lasting impression.

Ever felt overlooked? Invisible? Like a shadow?

Write your own story.
Share a time when you felt overlooked.

Have you ever felt unnoticed? Even by God?

One of our great heroes of the faith is Abram. God gave him a powerful promise and a high calling. All the people of the world were blessed because of him! But there's a person in Abram's life who often goes unnoticed: Hagar.

A minor player in the story of Abram, Hagar's role was not an enviable one. Growing impatient to receive the son God had promised, Abram and Sarai took matters into their own hands. Sarai had the not-so-bright idea to let Abram impregnate her maidservant, Hagar.

Newsflash: When you share your husband with the gal who works for you, and she gets pregnant just like you planned, you are going to be overwhelmed with jealousy. Duh.

The situation between Sarai and Hagar became so toxic that Hagar ended up running away into the desert. Escape from the Jerry Springer–like family drama held more appeal than staying in a place where she could deliver her baby.

The Bible tells us the angel of the Lord found her out in the middle of nowhere and approached her with kindness. Calling her by name, he asked her two simple questions: Where have you come from? Where are you going?

It was the simple acknowledgement that he knew she was out of place. She was not where she should have been. Even though she had escaped unnoticed, she had not escaped the notice of God.

The angel told her to name her son Ishmael (which means "God hears"), because the Lord had heard her cry of distress. Hagar responded by using another name to refer to the Lord in Genesis 16:13: El-Roi, the God Who

Sees Me.

Hagar points out a beautiful truth about God: No one goes unnoticed by the Lord! He hears and He sees.[16]

A guy in great distress is seen by God. The person who feels alone and forgotten is known by God. The girl who feels like a wallflower does not escape God's notice. The teen who disappears into the background is in God's focus. The student who is overlooked catches the gaze of God. The one who feels ignored has God's attention.

You are seen. You are known. You are noticed. You are the focus. You are gazed upon. You have His attention.

Grab a string,
and tie it into a bow.
Then tape it to this page so that you

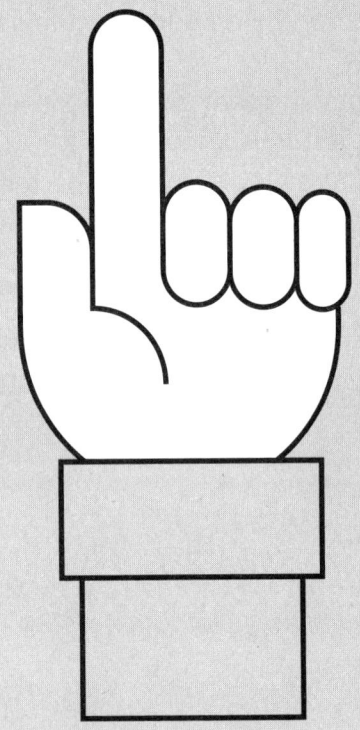

NEVER
FORGET.

You are seen. You are known. You are noticed.

You are the focus. You are gazed upon.

You have His attention.

Friendship isn't about who you've known the longest.
It's about who walked into your life and said,
"I'm here for you" and proved it.

—Unknown

Sometimes we understand that we are seen by God, but we feel overlooked by those around us. We are lonely and isolated.

King David knew a little bit about loneliness. In Psalm 142:4 he said,

> I look for someone to come and help me,
> but no one gives me a passing thought!
> No one will help me
> no one cares a bit what happens to me.

It is so easy to feel this way, especially when life is hard.

King David continued to cry out to God, knowing community could make an incredible difference in his life:

> Get me out of this dungeon
> so I can thank you in public.
> Your people will form a circle around me
> and you'll bring me showers of blessing! (Psalm 142:7, MSG)

When we allow the right people to circle around us, they bring strength, correction, and encouragement. Instead of the dry heat of standing alone, we will experience showers of blessing. We don't have to walk alone.

But how do we find this circle of people?

First, determine to be intentional. Don't sit for years being sad that you don't really have friends you can turn to, stop just waiting for relationships to magically happen and instead be intentional.

When I want to have a friend I can talk to regularly about things going on in life, I pick up the phone and start texting and messaging people. When I need a fun night out? I organize one. If I want to attend a *Stranger Things* watch party, I don't cross my fingers and hope to be invited to one. Instead, I buy a bunch of terrible-for-you food, Christmas lights, Eggo waffles and throw a party of my own. If I find myself jealous seeing Instagram photos of a group of people going out to dinner and a movie together, I dropped the envy, get proactive, and set up a movie night with that group.

Once I decided I was done just waiting to be invited and wallowing in my misery when I wasn't, I instead became an inviter. My relational world from that point forward began to transform. I started to develop a circle of friends who could bring the showers of blessing. They may or may not live in my neighborhood, city, or even state. But they will answer the phone before the sun rises if I need them. I will answer my phone for them, too.

Second, release yourself from the guilt and fear of forming friendships. I've been told hundreds of times to be careful about having a close group of friends so that you don't become a clique. If I choose to be in a close friendship with a few people, feelings will be hurt, people will feel rejected, and it will cause problems.

I'll be honest with you, every single one of those has proven true. I have unintentionally hurt people's feelings. I have made people feel rejected. And it has caused a boatload of problems. Boatloads.

I can let the guilt and fear of those things lock me in isolation or loneliness, or I can embrace the fact that I was created for community just like everyone else. I'm a better person when I have people who provide counsel and prayer in my life. I am a better student when I can get advice and cheerleading from other students. I'm a better daughter when I have friends who are encouraging me to keep my calendar filled with time with my family. I'm a better girl of faith when I can discuss the things of God with others. My belief is bolstered by the sharing of both blessing and struggle. And I'm a more compassionate human being when I'm being stretched to listen more to, care about, and pray for other people.

So I choose community. Not out of some whacky scheme to hurt other people but out of the pursuit to become a better version of me.

Write the names of the people you've invited into your circle.
Don't have names to write on those faces? That's okay. Write a
prayer below asking God to bring people into your life and circle.

Your new name is
KNOWN.
Affirm it below.

MY NAME IS

Known

15. Unforgivable

When you are a busy eight-year-old boy, you can find all kinds of trouble for yourself while playing outside. Sure, you can ride your bike, bounce a basketball, and write on the driveway with chalk. But what do you do when you've exhausted every bit of fun imaginable? You think of something a little crazy and a lot destructive.

One sunny fall afternoon, my brother decided he would create a rock-throwing contest for himself since he was bored with all of the normal activities. Struck with what can only be described as a stroke of brilliance, Ethan picked up some rocks, determined to see if he could throw them between our parents' cars.

And throw he did. Right into Mom's back windshield, which instantly shattered. Not just a crack—oh no. The windshield was demolished! That kid may not have great aim, but he can deliver a zinger of a pitch.

Right away, Ethan fessed up to Dad that he might, just possibly have made a teeny-tiny mistake.

My dad walked out, saw the missing windshield, and Pastor Jud left the building. What in the world was that little boy thinking?! My dad was fuming. An amazing lecture on irresponsibility and the enormous cost of this little mistake was welling up within him. After all, a new windshield wasn't exactly in the budget. As he stood and surveyed the damage, he heard some sniffling to the side and looked over to see tears streaming down Ethan's cheeks.

Then my little brother said, "I'm not worthy to be part of this family." He felt utterly unforgivable. What he had done was so huge, so terrible, and so epic, in his mind, that his actions seemed out of the realm of forgiveness.

Whether Ethan was brilliantly working his daddy to get out of trouble or he couldn't be more serious, Dad's heart broke as he looked at his boy. Who cares about a dumb windshield when your child needs to know he is loved and forgiven? Well, my mom might have cared a tiny bit the next time she was driving down the freeway, but that didn't matter nearly as much as Ethan. No doubt.

At some point in our lives, we've all busted the window with our mistakes.

Write one of those times on the broken window below. What have you done that haunts you and makes you feel like you're unforgivable?

Few of us question the forgiveness of God when it comes to our friends, family, and community. We are confident that the sacrifice of Jesus covers the sins and mistakes of those we love. Why wouldn't it?

But some of us, if we are gut-level honest, question the Lord's forgiveness in our own lives. We know the darkness in the deepest recesses of our souls. We are keenly aware of the mile-long list of our shortcomings and mistakes. We are intimately acquainted with selfish choices we've made and the people we've hurt.

We feel unforgivable.

Feeling exempt from the forgiveness of God is actually a strange form of pride. It is declaring that the perfect life and sacrificial death of Christ were somehow not good enough to account for the sins in our lives. That pride says our mistakes are too big to be encompassed by the forgiveness offered in Jesus. Believing we are unforgivable states that our sins hold more power than our God does.

Yikes. Is there any way we could really be beyond forgiveness?

On that fateful day of Jesus's crucifixion, He hung between two criminals. The Bible is not specific about the crimes of the two criminals nailed to crosses on each side of Jesus, but we do know a little bit about the one man who was released so that Jesus could be sacrificed instead. Luke tells us that Barabbas was "in prison for taking part in an insurrection in Jerusalem against the government, and for murder" (Luke 23:19).

When faced with the prospect of releasing one of the three criminals set to be crucified, the religious leaders petitioned for the release of Barabbas the murderer. It makes you wonder what crimes the other two criminals committed. Two men with death sentences, passed over for release. They must have been unforgivable.

Nope. Not quite.

One criminal, hands and feet nailed to a cross, soul hovering on the verge of hell, turned to face the Savior. Every word must have been pained, but he said, "Jesus, remember me when you come into your Kingdom" (Luke 23:42).

And Jesus—loving, merciful Jesus—replied, "I assure you, today you will be with me in paradise" (Luke 23:43).

Total, unquestionable forgiveness. There is not one sin, one mistake, or any terrible choice that is outside the amazing love, mercy, and forgiveness of Jesus. Not a single one.

Stop right here. Hold up for a second. Flip back over to that window you broke with your mistake. Read it again. Then rip that page out. Tear it up. Shred it to tiny bits. You are forgiven. There isn't one single thing that is outside of the grace and forgiveness of Jesus.

May 19, 1944. Twenty-one-year-old Howard Linn took off from an Allied airbase in England. As the bomber closed in on Brunswick, Germany, a group of 190 German fighters attacked. Hearing machine-gun rounds hit his plane, Linn noticed that one engine had burst into flame. The wing was quickly engulfed in fire. The time had come for Howard Linn to parachute out of the bomber.

As he dropped from twenty thousand feet, he passed through clouds and attempted to spot a landing. Once safely on the ground, he hid in a brush pile for the night while listening to the sounds of patrols looking for the airman who had abandoned his parachute.

Walking west, Linn eventually came to a small German village, where he was noticed by a fifteen-year-old boy, Wilfried Beerman. He followed the boy to his house, where he ate sandwiches and enjoyed coffee while the family decided what to do with the American. Having decided to turn Linn in to officials, Wilfried flagged down a police officer, who took the airman into custody.

For the next year, Howard Linn endured rough interrogations, suffered eighty-seven straight days of marching, and ate maggot-infested meat, all while one quarter of his fellow prisoners died due to dysentery and other ailments.

May 8, 1945. English soldiers rolled into camp, and Linn was again a free man.

Fifty years later, Linn connected once more with Wilfried Beerman, that teenage boy who had handed him over to the enemy. The now sixty-five-year-old Beerman expressed his deep feelings of guilt for turning Linn in to authorities, but Howard Linn responded with six simple words: "It was war. I forgive you."

And thus a beautiful friendship began. Linn returned to Germany to visit Beerman and his family. Every Christmas, Howard's family received a package filled with German chocolate and gifts. [17]

What a beautiful story of forgiveness! Linn could have easily been bitter and consumed with unforgiveness for all he had been through. Instead, he felt no condemnation for his new friend. None. Amazing.

No matter what you've done, no matter who you've hurt, no matter how you've sinned, there is no condemnation for you either. Romans 8:1 declares, "Now there is no condemnation for those who belong to Christ Jesus."

No condemnation. None. Amazing.

When we reach out to Jesus, confessing Him as our Lord and Savior, asking for His forgiveness and requesting that He pour His grace and mercy out on us, there is no condemnation. We belong to Him.

The cheating that grieves you? There is no condemnation. You belong to Christ.

The lying that haunts you? There is no condemnation. You belong to Christ.

The dishonesty that consumes you with guilt? There is no condemnation. You belong to Christ.

The betrayal that you deeply regret? There is no condemnation. You belong to Christ.

The addiction that has you in its grip? There is no condemnation. You belong to Christ.

When you are in Christ, loved by Christ, and forgiven by Christ, there is no condemnation. Now it is time to extend some grace and forgiveness to yourself.

Write a letter to yourself. Take a few moments to
extend grace and forgiveness to yourself.

Dear Self,

···

···

···

···

···

···

···

···

···

···

···

···

···

···

Your new name is
FORGIVEN.
Proclaim it below.

MY NAME IS

_____

Group Discussion Questions

1. Share two things God has done in the light that you need to remember when you are surrounded by darkness.

2. Are you running on empty or feeling full? What activities fill you up?

3. What can you do to start feeling more at home? How can you put down roots, plan long term and embrace your community?

4. Who is in your circle of people that brings you showers of blessing?

5. How have you broken the window in your life?

Session 4

16. Frazzled

My birthday was creeping up quickly, and I was not entirely sure what I wanted to do to celebrate. The previous year, I had thrown my birthday party at an escape room, and it was so much fun we finally decided to do another one. I knew going into it that this escape room was going to be a bit scarier, especially considering the number of waivers we had to sign, but I was still pumped. How scary could it actually be?

Joined by my mom and my four bravest friends, we pulled into an ominous building surrounded by a dark parking lot just off the Las Vegas Strip. Once our escape began, we found ourselves in a cramped hallway where we were told to pull the provided canvas bags over our heads. As soon as we were encased in darkness, I heard one of my friends scream as she was pulled away. If I wasn't frazzled already, I sure was at that moment. Soon, it was my turn to be quickly jerked away by some stranger into another room.

Pulling the bags off our heads, we started the frantic work of trying to escape. Twenty minutes later, we found a hole in the wall that led to a dingy, darkly lit bathroom. I creaked the bathroom door open and found a dirty, crazed girl chained to the wall. No joke. She was incredibly creepy. Not knowing how to get her free, I just left her to hang out there for a bit. I crawled back into the main room and went to work on the puzzles. What I didn't know was one of the other players had obtained a key and proceeded to UNLOCK the crazy lady from her chains.

I was innocently looking for clues when I heard my friend, Kira, scream. As I turned around, I saw Kira frantically crawling through the hole in the wall followed by the bloodied, frantic looking actor who then started running at us. Panic ensued.

Kira sprinted towards a wall and hid herself with her jacket, like toddlers who cover their eyes and hope they are hidden when playing Hide-And-Seek. I tripped and fell into a refrigerator that seemed to come out of nowhere. My mom accidentally punched a cabinet and immediately started bleeding. My other friends, Zoe, Kristen and Paloma, bolted in every direction away from the terrifying, mumbling lady. It took a few minutes for our hearts to start beating again.

Overwhelmed by anxiety and fear, I was one frazzled mess.

Tell your own frazzled story below.

Once upon a time...

At the end of an intense day of competitive surfing on Jeffreys Bay in South Africa, two finalists waited on the waves while hundreds of fans stood on the beach and cheered. Suddenly those cheers turned into terrified screams as a shark emerged from the water directly behind pro surfer Mick Fanning. Dragged underwater as the shark pulled his leg rope, Fanning started kicking and punching the shark.

Y'all. He punched Jaws in the face. Seriously.

Suddenly, Fanning's leg rope broke free. He swam for the shore, screaming for his competitor and friend, Julian Wilson, to turn and swim for safety. But Wilson, who had just watched his friend be pulled off his surfboard and underwater, was paddling straight for him, determined to use his board as a weapon to stab the shark if needed.[18]

Ever felt like the sharks were circling in the water? Maybe you are filled with anxiety about a conflict with a friend that seems to escalate with each day. Maybe you are overcome with worry for a sibling who is making all the wrong choices and breaking your parents' hearts. Maybe dread of an unknown future is dragging you down.

As the sharks circle, we can feel incredibly frazzled. So, how do we escape the sharks of life?

Lesson 1: Punch the shark in the face and swim away.

When worry and anxiety emerge in our lives, we have to learn to punch "frazzled" in the face. Our greatest weapon in that moment is prayer. The Bible is clear: "Cast all your anxiety on him because he cares for you" (1 Peter 5:7, NIV).

Cast all your anxiety on Jesus. All of it. Every single bit.

All your cares: The personal ones, the friendship ones, the family-related ones. The cares of the past, the present, and the future. The cares of your school, your church, and your country. The cares of the financial pressure you carry, the worry for your family you shoulder, and the health concerns you hold.

Sometimes when we lift our cares to God, they seem to fall right back in our laps. What do we do then? We hand them right back over. We start to feel frazzled again. We reach out to the Lord in prayer and give Him our worries once more. We are consumed afresh with anxiety. We pray. We pray. We pray.

It is like the most wonderful game of Hot Potato ever.

Fear lands in our laps. We toss it back to God. Anxiety hits our hands. We hold it out to Jesus. Frazzled consumes our hearts. We throw it to the Lord. Over and over and over again. And each time we hand it to God, it takes a bit longer to find its way back to us.

Yes, punching our anxiety in the face with prayer will go a long way in helping us feel less frazzled. But that's not the only lesson we can pick up from our shark-fighting surfer friends.

What has you feeling frazzled? What anxieties are trying to pull you under? Write them on the shark fins below.

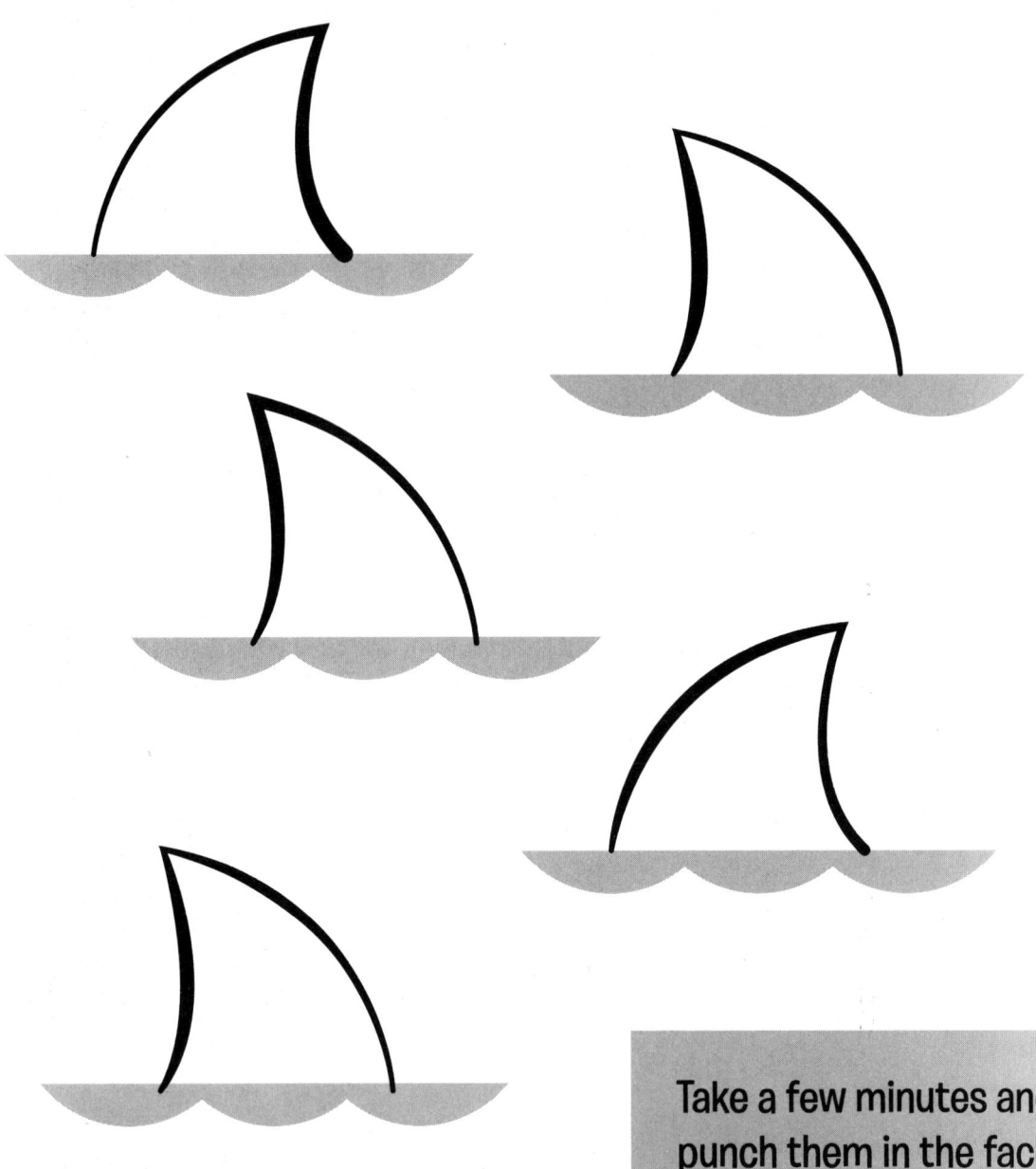

Take a few minutes and punch them in the face with some prayer.

Lesson 2: Be willing to ask for and accept help.

When Julian Wilson witnessed the shark attack, he started paddling toward his friend to help instead of heading to the beach for safety. Talk about courage. Or craziness! Either way, when fear and anxiety are on the attack, we could really use some help.

In our frazzled times, we might need to call in some reinforcements. We need to ask for and accept help when necessary. Yes, letting people into the anxiety and stress of our personal lives can leave us feeling vulnerable. But as one of the characters says on Supergirl (yes, I watch Supergirl— move along): "The thing that makes [people] strong is that we have the guts to be vulnerable. We have the ability to feel the depths of our emotion, and we know that we will walk through it to the other side."[19]

It takes guts to be vulnerable, but sometimes we need help walking to the other side of our fears. Being open and honest with friends and family can go a long way in helping us cope with the sharks circling in our lives.

There are also times when we need to seek the counsel of a pastor or professional. Some of us, though, have a long list of excuses to stay away from a counselor. At the top of the list, we may feel like we simply can't afford counseling. Our family can't afford the bill. We can't afford the gossip. We can't afford the time. We. Just. Can't. Afford. It.

But when your family has you frazzled. When you're anxious about school. When you're consumed with fear about your health. When you're distressed about nasty dating drama. When you're worried about a friend's betrayal, you simply can't afford not to go to counseling.

There is no shame in accepting help when the sharks are circling. In fact, it may be the most powerful thing you can do when you feel frazzled.

Need help?

Take a minute to call your church to see if they can recommend a counselor, or hop online and search for a Christian counselor.

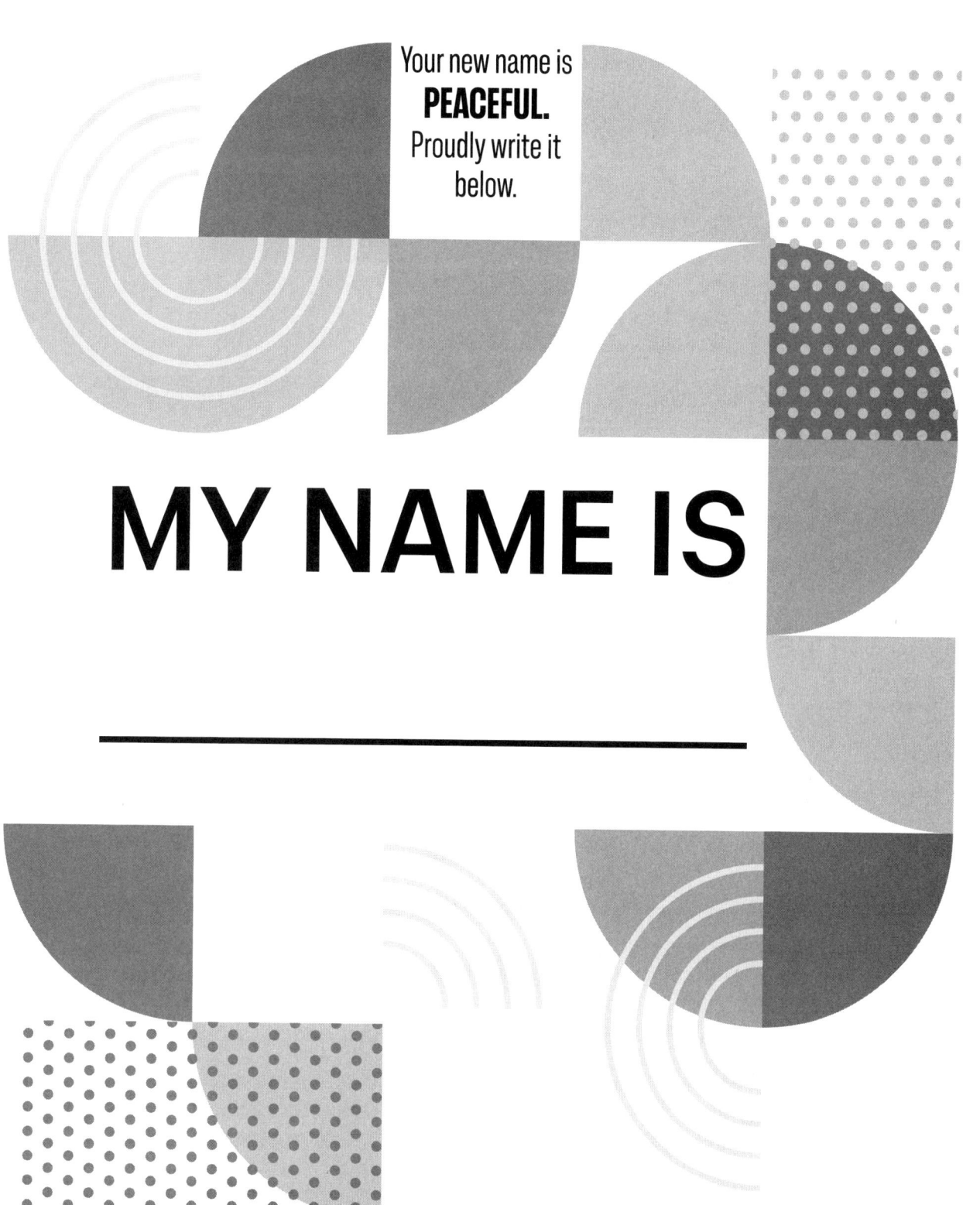

Your new name is
PEACEFUL.
Proudly write it
below.

MY NAME IS

_____

17. Overwhelmed

Overwhelmed.

I simply felt overwhelmed. There weren't major life changes that did me in. No, these were little, everyday events that left me exhausted without my even realizing it.

"Can you give me some help with our class assignment, Emma?"

"Sis, I need you to clean your room before our guests come over."

"Hey, babe, the tire on your car has a nail in it. You need to have someone take a look at it."

"Can I call you this week? I want to ask your advice about something."

"We need a lunch date. I feel like I haven't seen you in months!"

"Emma, can you give me a ride to school."

"You need to stay after school for that extra rehearsal."

"Can you volunteer at church on Saturday?"

"Would you sing at an event we have coming up?"

That overwhelmed feeling haunted me from the moment my eyes opened in the morning to the moment they closed while trying to finish up work on my couch at night.

I felt just like the Cat in the Hat with his carefully balanced treasures on his head, tail, and hands.[20]

> Look
> I can hold up the cup
> And the milk and the cake!
> I can hold up these books!
> And the fish on a rake!
> I can hold the toy ship
> And a little toy man!

Then the Cat and all his toys came crashing down. I, too, was in danger of falling flat on my head, and my carefully balanced things would certainly fall.

What are you trying to balance in your life and family right now?

Write those things in the items below.

How close are you to having all the things fall?

too close

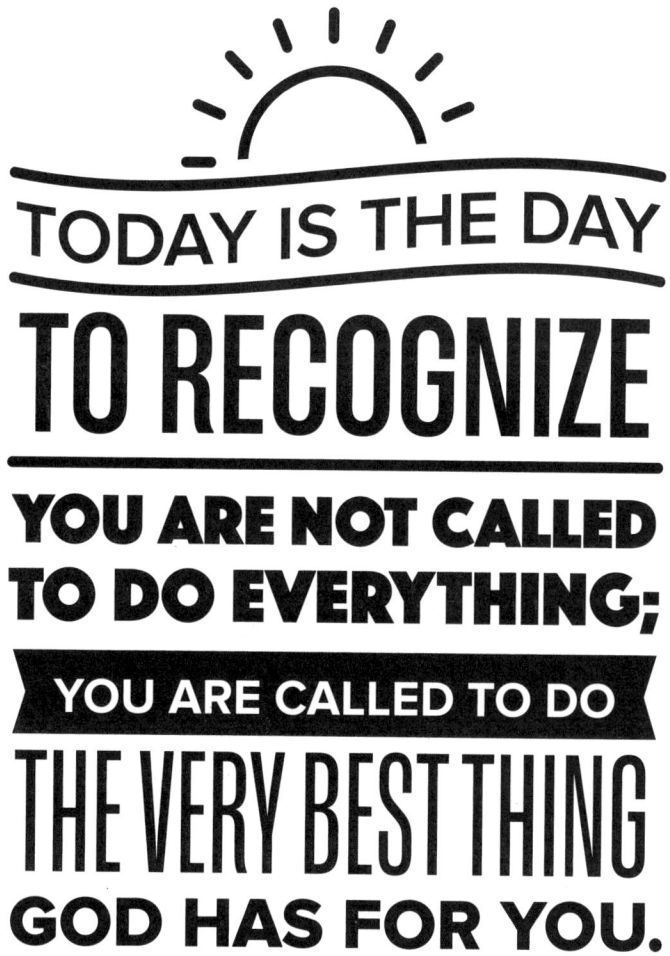

TODAY IS THE DAY
TO RECOGNIZE
YOU ARE NOT CALLED
TO DO EVERYTHING;
YOU ARE CALLED TO DO
THE VERY BEST THING
GOD HAS FOR YOU.

—Tiffany Cooper

We've balanced some stuff, you guys. We're willing to bet you have too.

But balancing boatloads of stuff is exhausting. Our spindly little arms get tired.

The homework. The extracurriculars. The job. The friends. The parents. The volunteering. The hobbies. The housework. The tests. The siblings. The church. The fun.

Whew! We feel worn out just thinking about it.

It's all wonderful. Well, let's be real, not the math homework. There's nothing wonderful about math homework. I loathe math. The rest is pretty great, though. Even though we balance things we love (and a few things we don't), it can be so stinkin' tiring.

Two things that will make us feel bone-weary when our arms are loaded down: the weight we carry and the pace at which we move.

First, we have to address the weight of the things we carry. We are experts at balancing many things at one time, but eventually the weight will become too much to hold.

We overstuff our calendars and overcommit ourselves by saying yes to too many things. Feelings of guilt, fear of disappointing others, and the need to be needed keep us from saying no. We have to learn to say, "No!"

Saying no is a necessity in order to manage the weight we carry so we won't find ourselves overwhelmed. Oh, but it is so hard sometimes to tell people no.

There was a time when, if I was asked to volunteer for something or attend a school event, I felt it necessary to launch into a well-crafted, multipoint defense of why I needed to say no. In order to not hurt someone's feelings or justify my absence, I would lawyer up and bring my best case forward. I then heard something a pastor's wife, Kay Warren, told my mom, "No is an okay word to say. You don't have to defend those kinds of choices to everybody in an effort to make them happy."

What?! You can just say no and that's it? That's right. With a smile and a gracious spirit, you can look at people and just say, "No, I'm not going to be able to do that." That's it. How incredibly freeing is that?

Can you come to our Christmas party? I'm sorry. I'm not going to be able to attend.

Can you attend the graduation parties of this year's Seniors? I really wish I could, but I'm not able to be there.

Can you stop by my study group ... club meeting ... birthday party? *insert sweet smile* Nope ... Can't make it ... Sorry.

Learning the art of saying no is an absolute game changer. No makes the weight you carry sustainable for the long haul.

Instead of a To-Do List, create a

STOP DOING LIST

What do you need to say no to?

- [ ] hanging out w/people when I have hw.
- [ ] helping people revise their papers
- [ ] giving people answers
- [ ] biting off more than I can chew constantly.
- [ ]
- [ ]
- [ ]
- [ ]

While managing the weight of the things we carry, it is also vital to take a long look at the pace at which we are moving.

We can run hard and move at a breakneck speed for a season, but eventually we will find ourselves worn out, stretched too thin, and flat-out overwhelmed. We simply cannot function at our best when we are weary. We cannot be at our best for God if we are not first refreshed by Him. He says,

> I'll refresh tired bodies;
> I'll restore tired souls. (Jeremiah 31:25, MSG)

Tired body? Check. Tired Soul? Check.

Refreshment and restoration sound like they're right up my alley.

We're reminded of hiking. Now, we are no experts on hiking, but even we know you can't keep the same pace all the time when tromping through the woods. If the terrain is flat and easy, you can move your feet at a pretty fast clip. But when the hills are steep, the path is littered with boulders, or there are branches to duck under at every turn, you have to adjust your pace.

The speed at which you can run when you're in the first weeks of the school year is very different from your speed when you are in the middle of finals.

The rate at which you move when you're in school and working part time is not the same as your pace when you've reached glorious summer break.

The pace you can keep when you are nine is quite altered when you're in your teens. And is bound to be different when you're a twenty-something or, dare I say, even older.

If we are going to find relief from being overwhelmed, we have to adjust our pace to make sure we have time for the most important thing. If we are not careful, the supersonic speed of our lives will swallow the time of rejuvenation and refreshment we need that can only be found in time with Jesus. With so many things vying for our attention, we can have a hard time carving out time with the Lord.

I love the way The Message describes our time with God in Psalm 23:3:

> True to your word,
>> you let me catch my breath
>> and send me in the right direction.

When we take the time to slow our pace, connect with Jesus, and catch our breaths, we can take on whatever the day may bring.

Seasons will come and go. Busy and relaxed. Good and bad. Heavy and light. Quick and slow. When we choose to shed some of the weight we carry, slow our pace, and fill ourselves with God, we won't be overwhelmed.

MY FANTASY DAY

8 a.m. _____

9 a.m. _____

10 a.m. _____

11 a.m. _____

12 a.m. _____

1 p.m. _____

2 p.m. _____

3 p.m. _____

4 p.m. _____

5 p.m. _____

6 p.m. _____

7 p.m. _____

8 p.m. _____

9 p.m. _____

10 p.m. _____

Find ways to make
this happen more often!

Your new name is
REFRESHED.
Write it below.

MY NAME IS

Refreshed

18. Selfish

Inside each one of us is a kingdom where we sit on the throne. I call it the Kingdom of Me. The world is primarily messed up because it's full of people all operating from the Kingdom of Me, all looking out for their own interests and not the interests of others.

—Kay Warren

In the Kingdom of Me, we don't do the outdoors. In the Kingdom of Me, crazy adventures should be enjoyed while holding a tub of popcorn and sitting in a movie theater. In the Kingdom of Me, vacations should be spent in sun-soaked cities, exploring, shopping, and wandering art museums. In the Kingdom of Me, it's flip-flops over hiking boots every day of the week. In the Kingdom of Me, all things ice, snow, and cold should be avoided at all costs.

Enter one sneaky little invader called a choir trip. At school one day, my director presented us with a packet laying out the opportunity to perform with our choir in Reykjavik, Iceland. You read that right: Iceland.

Ten months later, my mom and I filled our suitcases with gloves, fur-trimmed coats, and *gasp* hiking boots. We hopped on a plane and headed to the Land of Fire and Ice. Lots and lots of ice. And we embarked on one crazy outdoor adventure. We went glacier hiking.

Why would the queens of the Kingdom of Me violate the clearly stated laws of the land?

Well. I love great photo-ops more than I dislike the outdoors. I love time with my friends and my mom more than I hate hiking boots. And I love having adventurous stories to tell more than I loathe ice, snow, and cold.

So we laced up the hiking boots and donned the waterproof hiking pants. We strapped on shoe spikes and very unfashionable helmets. We took hold of ice axes, and we started climbing. On a glacier. In nineteen-degree weather.

If we had not allowed an invasion of the Kingdom of Me, we would have missed out on a huge, bucket-list kind of adventure.

What are the rules in the Kingdom of You? Write the "Thou Shalt" and the "Thou Shalt Nots" on the scroll below.

thats a lot of work

Why is it so hard to set ourselves aside and put others first? To put someone else's needs and wants above our own?

Three little words in Philippians 2:3 square things up quickly: "Don't be selfish."

So simple. So incredibly complicated.

Because we like things the way we like them. We want things the way we want them. We want things to happen in our time frame, in our style, with our preferences taken into account.

Selfishness comes as naturally to us as blinking. We may no longer hit our friends when they take our toy from us, like we did when we were toddlers. These days our selfishness is dressed up in big-kid outfits.

When someone steals the parking spot that we clearly had our blinker on to claim, we shoot them the look. You know the one. The. Look.

When you see a sink stacked full of dirty dishes, and instead of taking five minutes to rinse them and stick them in the dishwasher, you add one more and run away before anyone sees. You're intent on catching up on YouTube videos. Surely someone else will take care of the dishes.

When one person says they're going to write their name on one bag of pizza rolls and your name on the other bag of pizza rolls so that you don't have to share, then backs out of the deal and eats both bags instead … oh, wait. It's my brother who does that. Yeah. Selfish.

sigh But, alas, Paul lays it out. Don't be selfish.

And he doesn't end there. He says, "Do nothing out of selfish ambition or vain conceit. Rather, in humility value others above yourselves, not looking to your own interests but each of you to the interests of the others"

(Philippians 2:3-4, NIV).

Wait. Hang on just a second. You mean we need to not just think about how our words or actions benefit jus, but we need to look to the interests of our families, classmates, friends, church family, and strangers?

Oh man. We're going to need to hop off the throne of the Kingdom of Me so that we can value others above ourselves. Even though it feels cozy to sink back on the cushions of our thrones, we must learn how to humble ourselves.

Jot down all the things you should do out of selfish ambition.

"Do nothing out of selfish ambition or vain conceit. Rather, in humility value others above yourselves, not looking to your own interests but each of you to the interests of the others" (Philippians 2:3-4, NIV).

Oh yeah, Nothing. And nothing means nothing.

Selflessness really hinges on one powerful word: humility.

Humility is not the degrading and belittling of yourself. Instead, humility is the courteous respect of God and others.

Let's look at the one person who has modeled that kind of humility at its finest. Philippians 2 charges on with these compelling words:

You must have the same attitude that Christ Jesus had.

> Though he was God,
> > he did not think of equality with God
> > as something to cling to.
> Instead, he gave up his divine privileges;
> > he took the humble position of a slave
> > and was born as a human being.
> When he appeared in human form,
> > he humbled himself in obedience to God
> > and died a criminal's death on a cross.
>
> Therefore, God elevated him to the place of highest honor
> > and gave him the name above all other names,
> that at the name of Jesus every knee should bow,
> > in heaven and on earth and under the earth,
> and every tongue declare that Jesus Christ is Lord,
> > to the glory of God the Father. (Philippians 2:5-11)

We should have the same attitude as Christ. Whoa. That's a heavy charge. You mean we're supposed to be like Jesus who gave up His divine, royal privileges so we could be restored to a relationship with the Lord and for the glory of God the Father?

Yep. That's exactly it.

attitude

noun at·ti·tude \'a-tə-ˌtüd, -ˌtyüd\

a : a mental position with regard to a fact or state

b : a feeling or emotion toward a fact or state

Jot down every adjective you can think of to
describe the attitude of Christ
Go ahead.
Write every single word you can think of.

Now go and adopt the same attitude of Christ Jesus.

Your new name is
SELFLESS.
Declare it below.

MY NAME IS

Selfless

19. Failed Family

Not too long ago my mom was heading out of town, and I wanted to get some snacks before I went off to camp for the week. I knew I would hate going alone, so I asked my dad to come with me. He informed me that he would only come with me if I joined him in his ventures to buy some gym equipment that he could shove into our guest room.

I reluctantly agreed and tagged along for the 30 minute car ride. Once we got there, he observed all the equipment for at least an hour mumbling, "Ooh, my wife wouldn't like that. What can I do my pull-ups on? These weights are kind of ugly, what else is there?"

It felt like an eternity as I wandered around the strange-smelling workout contraptions. When he finally figured out what he wanted, he asked when the shop owner could make the delivery. Everything could be delivered within the hour. Unsurprisingly, my dad was very excited and jumped into the car to rush home to prepare the guest room, totally forgetting our deal.

I had a few expectations of our trip, and none of them involved me being forced into helping my dad move furniture out of the guest room. I expected to get my snacks and get some much needed rest, but instead, I ended up waiting all day before my dad remembered my previously promised food. My expectations exploded in my face.

I have expectations of our family as well. I somehow amassed expectations of family perfection throughout my life. Maybe it was watching problems solved in a quick half hour, with sappy music in the background and a well-timed parental discussion like on Full House reruns. Thank you, Tanner family. Or maybe I thought that a little life lesson filmed in a selfie-video would make every day great as long as it ended with, "Good luck, Charlie!" Whatever the case, I had expectations of what a perfect family looked like.

We certainly aren't the perfect family. We have all made plenty of mistakes. I sure do love my family, but we seem to slide off the path of perfection on a regular basis. I've been known to get frustrated and yell at my parents. It is possible I might have gotten in a fight or two with my brother. And maybe, just maybe, I've had a hug or two rejected along the way. Wow, so rude.

Draw your family here.

Nothing can hit us as deeply as the wounds that happen inside our homes. The moments we feel inadequate, discouraged, or like we failed in our role as a brother or sister, son or daughter. These are the relationships that mean the most to us. Our families are the ones with whom we can let down our walls and show our true selves. Our home is the place where our hearts are most exposed.

Failing at school can hurt, because we are embarrassed or frustrated about what we did. However, when we feel like we have failed with the people we love the most in this world, the hurt comes not because of what we did but because of who we are. Again, nothing can hit us as deep as the wounds that happen inside our homes.[21]

When our family expectations and perfection are derailed, we assign ourselves the name Failure. But what if perfection wasn't the goal?

I stumbled upon an incredible article from a mom, Jess, at wonderoak.com capturing the truth that, while we may not be perfect in our families, we are enough.[22]

> I'm not perfect, but I am enough... and so are you.
>
> I enjoy them enough.
>
> Sometimes I smell their hair and I kiss their cheeks. I laugh at their jokes and I marvel that I am so blessed. Time stops in moments like that and everything is perfect and worth it.
>
> Other times I am unsure if I will survive the hours of 4:00-8:30 pm, and if one can die of overexposure to bickering. One can. I'm sure of it.
>
> I enjoy them enough.

I love that, because I'm not perfect either. But I think I'm enough too.

I'm good enough at cleaning my room. Sometimes my floor is sparkly clean, and you could eat directly off of it. Of course, I wouldn't let you, because you'd mess it up. Duh. Sometimes my desk is spotless and completely organized. And sometimes my bed is made, and everything looks like it could grace the pages of a magazine.

Other times my floors are covered with dirty clothes and old school papers. Dirty dishes are stacked on every available surface. My bed is unmade because I'll be crashing back into it soon enough anyway. So why bother?

I'm good enough at cleaning my room.

I love my family enough. I love them when they are so preoccupied with their phones they miss what I've been trying to say for the last five minutes. I love them when they write embarrassing comments on my Instagram. I love them when they steal my food directly off my plate. I love them when they incessantly ask me if I'm doing my homework. I love them when they demolish me at board games. I love them when they try to cuddle on the couch even though I'm no longer five years old.

I love them. I adore them. I am crazy about them. I am incredibly fond of them. I absolutely cherish them.

I am not a perfect daughter or sister. But I do love them enough. Which makes everything else I do enough as well.

You may not be perfect, but you are enough.

There is no way to be the perfect son or daughter, brother or sister, but there are a million ways to be a good one.

Plaster the wall below with graffiti. Write a million ways you can build a good family.

WHAT CAN YOU DO TO PROMOTE WORLD PEACE? GO HOME AND LOVE YOUR FAMILY.

—Mother Teresa

We don't always get it right, but we can be faithful to do our best for the family God has given us. We will not walk in perfection, but we can strive to love them well, accept them fully, and lift them up continually. We may not be bringing home the Person of the Year trophy anytime soon, but we can imperfectly urge our family on to become all God created them to be.

My mom's friend Julie Richard of FearlessMom.com reminds her often that every member of our family was created "on purpose, with a purpose, and for a purpose."

One of the things that my brother says about me on a pretty constant loop around our house is "What is wrong with her?!" In case you are wondering, fourteen-year-old boys don't understand seventeen-year-old girls at all.

He will walk into our bathroom, and it will look like makeup and hair products have exploded everywhere. He can hardly find his lone deodorant and toothbrush, and he will say, "What is wrong with her?!"

Seemingly out of nowhere, my tears will start flowing. The girl drama might just be amping up a tad bit, and he will say, "What is wrong with her?!"

He goes to the pantry to find something to eat and will come storming through the kitchen saying, "What is wrong with her?! You don't take a man's Cinnamon Toast Crunch."

And my mom reminds him, "There is nothing wrong with her. She is just wired up differently than you. Sorry to inform you, but you may never fully understand your sister, or any other girl for that matter. But you can understand this: God created, designed, and knit her together on purpose."

In fact, Psalm 139:13-14 declares,

> You made all the delicate, inner parts of my body

and knit me together in my mother's womb.
Thank you for making me so wonderfully complex!

You are God-created, designed, and knit together on purpose. Our family members are God-created, designed, and knit together on purpose. Those ruggedly handsome good looks? On purpose. That quirky personality? On purpose. That strong will? On purpose. That amazing imagination? On purpose.

We are also created with the purpose of being in a deep, meaningful relationship with God.

When we understand we are all created with the purpose of worshiping and connecting with Jesus, it without a doubt drives the decisions we make and the actions we take. In fact, we can join David's cry in Psalm 139:1-6:

> O Lord, you have examined my heart
>   and know everything about me.
> You know when I sit down or stand up.
>   You know my thoughts even when I'm far away.
> You see me when I travel
>   and when I rest at home.
>   You know everything I do.
> You know what I am going to say
>   even before I say it, Lord.
> You go before me and follow me.
>   You place your hand of blessing on my head.
> Such knowledge is too wonderful for me,
>   too great for me to understand!

When we begin to truly believe we are created with the purpose of worshiping and connecting, everything changes. Those chores you're doing for the millionth time is an opportunity for you to thank God for your parents. The hang-out time on the couch is an opportunity to remind your family how much Jesus loves them. Coffee and chat time with a friend is a chance to help them see that God is with them and for them. We can encourage our parents, siblings, and friends that they are created to worship and be in relationship with Jesus.

Finally, God has given each one of us gifts, talents, and passions He can use to accomplish the purposes He has set out before us. He has created us for a purpose.

One of our greatest jobs in our families is to help them pull that truth deep into their hearts and lives. I need to help them grasp that God has created them for an incredible purpose.

I can't do it alone. Our whole family needs to come together and understand we were each created on purpose - God created, designed, and knit together.

We need to encourage each other to grasp that we were created with a purpose to discover a deep, meaningful relationship with Jesus.

We need to declare that we were created for a purpose and help one another discover our gifts and talents and how we can use them.

Yes, we were all created on purpose, with a purpose, and for a purpose. And we can help our families draw this truth deeply into their hearts and lives.

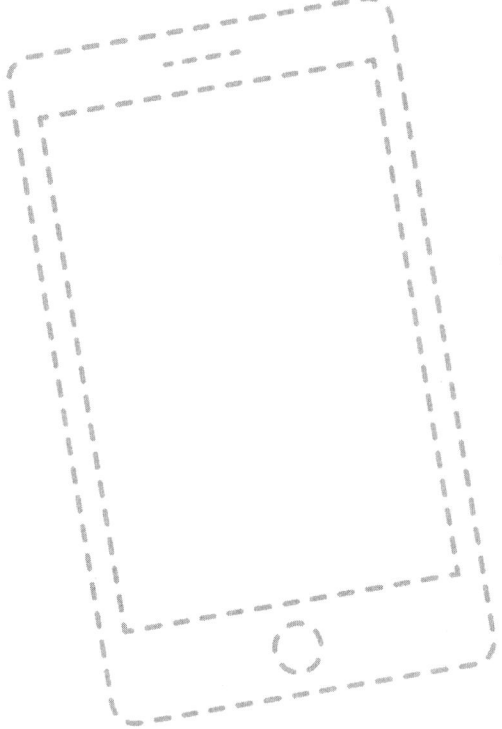

Grab your phone.

Text your family.

parents.

siblings.

Let them know they're created on purpose,

with a purpose

and for a purpose.

Your new name is
ON PURPOSE.
Claim it proudly
it below.

MY NAME IS

_____

20. Ready to Quit

I almost fractured my skull tripping and driving my face into a metal doorframe.

I sprained my elbow trying to master a pogo stick.

I broke my foot running the dreaded mile at school.

My mom stress-fractured her right foot pretending she was a prima ballerina.

She broke her left ankle running down a hill on a mission trip in Mexico.

She fractured her kneecap trying to snow-ski.

She chipped her wrist and broke her arm falling off our stage at church.

She tore the rotator cuff in her shoulder simply running down the sidewalk.

She almost broke her neck in a failed back-flip attempt on a trampoline.

We are accidents waiting to happen. So we quit.

We hereby resign from all things active and athletic. We give up working out. We hang up our snow skis, our running shoes, and our hiking boots. We abandon the opportunity to try anything exercise related. We'll cease using weights and treadmills. We officially terminate our involvement in any sport of any kind. Yes, that means you, too, bowling.

It's too hard. Too exhausting. And, frankly, too painful. We quit.

Ever want to quit? To throw in the towel? To walk away? Does it simply feel too draining, too difficult, and too painful? I get it. I really do. But we can't quit. Giving up isn't what's best for us.

If I want to be healthy, I can't resign from all things active and athletic. I have to still spend some quality time with my PE teacher forcing me to lift weights and sweat it out doing burpees even though they are of the devil. If I want to keep devouring brownies, my aerobics teacher and I need lots of hang-out time. I must continue to try something athletic and new and occasionally break out those hiking boots so I don't miss out on adventures with my friends. And I can't swear off all sports, although bowling, you're still on the outs.

Whatever God has called you to, you cannot quit! Until He releases you, keep strapping on those running shoes. Even when you're tired, worn out, and feel like you can't take another step, keep on going!

WHEN YOU TAKE GOD
OUT OF THE EQUATION
**AND START TO DO THINGS
IN YOUR OWN POWER,**
YOU WILL FIND YOURSELF IN A PLACE OF
ABSOLUTE DEPLETION.

—Tiffany Cooper

**Write a resignation letter.
What do you want to quit?**

Now write **"VOID"** in huge letters across your
resignation. You can't quit yet!

What you and I need is a good, healthy dose of persistence. Some stick-to-it-iveness. A batch of tenacity.

One Christmas Eve, during the last of nine thousand services, my mom's phone started relentlessly buzzing. Sitting in her usual front-row spot, she tried to slyly sneak a peek at her phone. My brother was calling. And calling. And calling.

Having attended Christmas services the day before, my brother and I were home alone on Christmas Eve. *cue Macaulay Culkin*

Flooded with a little bit of worry and a whole lot of mommy-guilt, Mom quickly texted him back. This is what ensued:

Mom: I'm in church. You ok? What do you need?

Ethan: Food aka Mac Donald chicken nuggets

Mom: Find something at home babe. We won't be home for at least another hour.

Ethan: There's nothin

Ethan: Literally nothin

Mom: Yes there is sweetie. You can find something.

Ethan: Plz mom

Ethan: Pleeeeeeessssssssssseeeeee mmmmmmmmoooooooooommmmmmmmm

Mom: Babe. We are tired. And won't be home for a while. Try to find something. Have a peanut butter toasted sandwich.

(My mom would like to quickly interrupt this regularly scheduled program to let you know that she is not normally so sweet and patient. But you guys, her kids were home alone. On Christmas Eve. Mommy guilt. So much mommy guilt. Proceed.)

Ethan: I need food

Mom: We have food. Even if it isn't your favorite. We have stuff.

Ethan:

Ethan: No we don't

Ethan: Please

Mom: We will have lots of pizza and eggs and bacon tomorrow. Have PB&J tonight.

(Pause, please. Pizza for Christmas dinner? Um. Yeah. While you enjoy ham or beautifully cooked turkey, my family scarfs down deep-dish pizza. All day. It's awesome. Continue on.)

Ethan: Plz mom!!!!!!!!!!!!!!

Ethan: Donald's chicken

Mom: No sweetie. I love you. I can make you a grilled cheese when I get home.

Ethan: Plz mom

Ethan: Dghsthdhbdycfyfd I'm hungry

Ethan: Gydggetyhfftghh

Mom: Sorry honey.

Ethan: Food

Ethan: Plz

Mom: No babe. I need to go because I'm in church. I love you.

Ethan: Wait

Ethan: U said grilled cheese we don't have that

Mom: We have some cheese that will work.

Ethan: Plllllll z zzzzz

Ethan: No we don't

Mom: Yes we do. I need to go. I love you.

Ethan: That's gross.

(Now, I'm going to assume he is saying the cheese is gross and not my mom's "I love you." At this point, someone should have given her a much-needed talking-to about discipline and such. But again, mom guilt. It is a powerful force, I tell you.)

Ethan: Food

Ethan: Food

Ethan: Food food food food food food food food food

Ethan: Plz

Ethan: Mom food

The phone now starts buzzing again.

Mom: I can't answer the phone.

The phone buzzes more.

Mom: I can't answer.

Once again, a phone call.

Mom: Dad is preaching. I can't talk.

Ethan: Foooooood

Ethan: Food

Mom: No. Go find something.

buzz, buzz, buzz

Mom: Stop calling honey.

Ethan: Not until food.

Ethan: Mom

Sanity finally prevailed. Mom powered her phone off and dropped it into the deep recesses of her purse.

But that, my friends, is tenacity. When we feel ready to throw in the towel, we need to channel that same level of perseverance.

Want to quit? Feel burned out? Have a text conversation with Jesus. Let Him know why you want to check out.

JC

I know, sweetie. I know you're tired. But you hang in there!

Stick in there. Don't walk out now. You've got this!

We aren't calling it a day just yet. Keep going. Keep going. Keeeeeeep Gooooing!

Don't quit now. My blessing is right around the corner.

A final thought from my mom:

I was tired.

I wished I wasn't. But I was.

While I was driving in my car—my best thinking spot—Galatians 6:9 kept running through my head: "Let's not get tired of doing what is good. At just the right time we will reap a harvest of blessing if we don't give up."

I prayed, "Lord, I'm not tired of doing good. I'm tired of criticism. I'm tired of disunity. I'm tired of betrayal. I'm just plain tired."

And I threw myself a big ol' pity party, complete with streamers and confetti. I shed a few tears, since it was my party and I could cry if I wanted to.

Then I heard the Lord whisper to me:

"Do not get tired of doing good to those who criticize you. Do not get tired of doing good to those who have created disunity. Do not get tired of doing good to those who may betray you. Do not get tired of doing good, period."

And the pity party came to a screeching halt. It was time to take a deep breath. Pull the big-girl pants up, stick it out, and not grow weary.

Why? Because "at just the right time we will reap a harvest of blessing if we don't give up."

If. Did you catch that? What a sneaky little word. If.

That blessing may not have come yesterday. And it might not come today or tomorrow. But in God's "just right time" it will come … if.

If I don't give up.
If I don't quit.
If I stick it out.
If I stay the course.
If I keep doing what is good.

So I will continue on.

I will keep doing good to those who criticize me.

I will keep doing good to those who have created disunity.

I will keep doing good to those who have betrayed me.

I will keep doing good.

When you go through deep waters,

I will be with you.

When you go through rivers of difficulty,

you will not drown.

When you walk through the fire of oppression,

you will not be burned up;

the flames will not consume you.

—Isaiah 43:2

SLIDES & STEPS

The goal of the game is to get to the blessing. No matter how hard it is, no matter how many slides you must go down, no matter how long it takes, GET TO THAT BLESSING.

RULES

1. Roll the dice. Move forward the number of spaces shown on the single die.

2. If you land at the bottom of the steps, just step on up to the space at the top of the ladder. Sometimes it's hard to climb steps, but it's totally worth it when you get to the top!

3. If you land at the top of a slide, that's a bummer! You've got to slide down to the bottom and continue on. Keep on going. You aren't defeated. Push on toward that blessing.

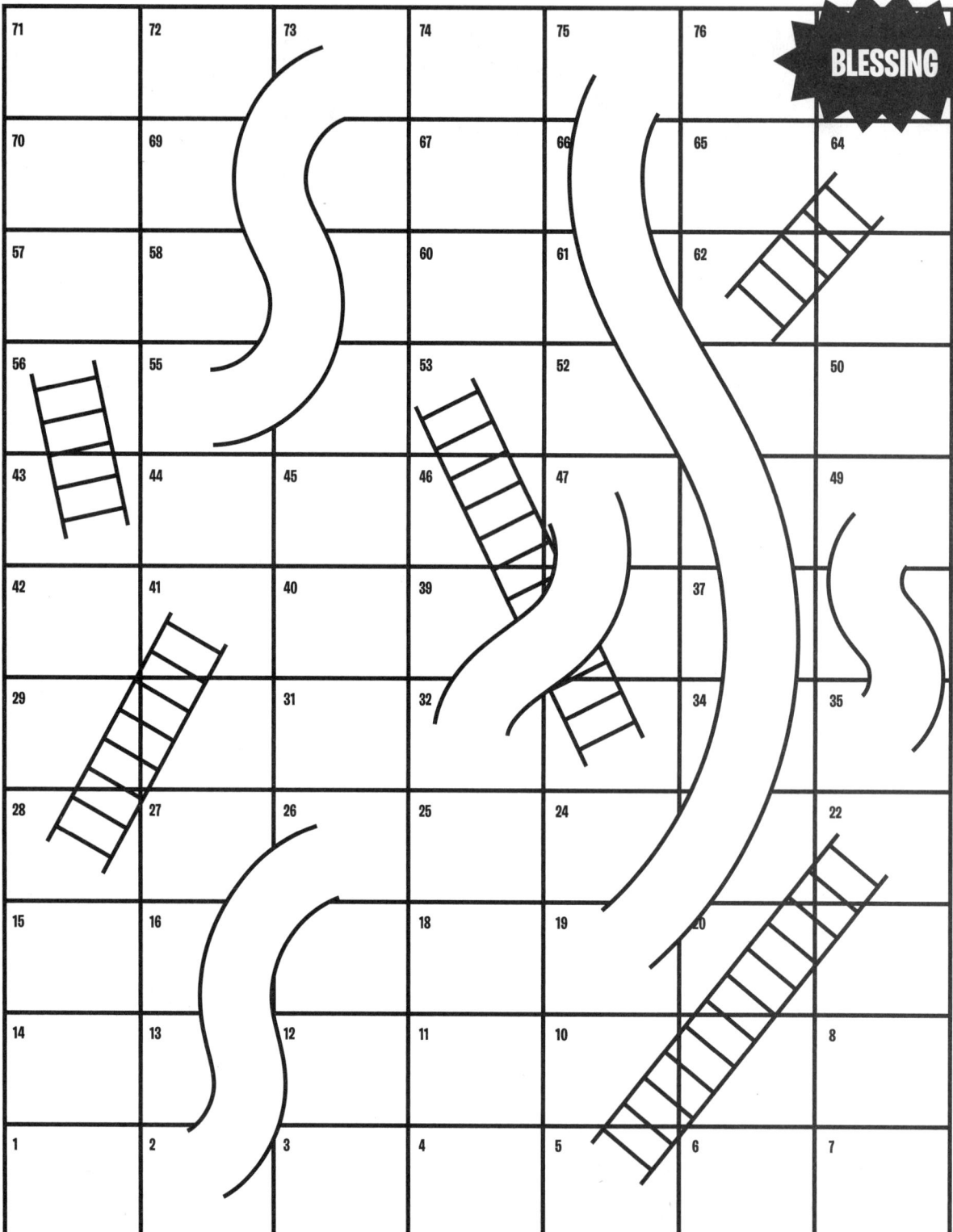

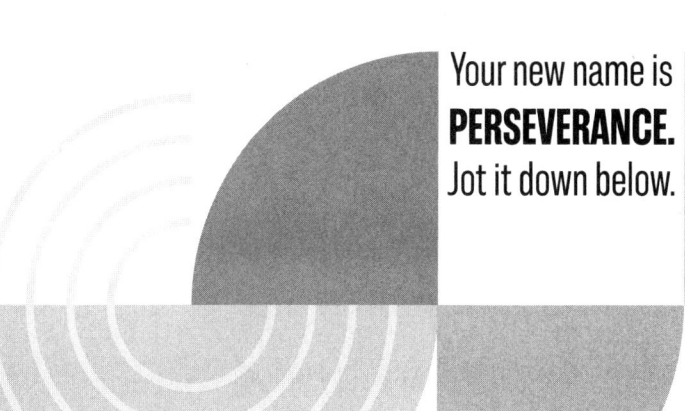

Your new name is
PERSEVERANCE.
Jot it down below.

MY NAME IS

_____

Group Discussion Questions

1. What sharks are circling and causing you to feel anxious?

2. Name three things that are at the top of your sTOp DOing list. What steps are you going to take to start crossing them off your list?

3. What are a few of the rules in the Kingdom of You?

4. We aren't perfect, but we can work to build a good family. Share one thing you do to help build your family.

5. What is an area of your life where you could use a healthy dose of persistence, some stick-to-it-iveness, and a batch of tenacity?

Take yourself on a coffee date. As you sip your latte, think about how you are feeling right this moment. How are you doing in these different areas of your life? Rank yourself on the latte scale. Color in the cups according to how you feel in each area.

Qualified		Restored	
Authentic		Chosen or Confident	
Strong		Special	
Enough		Unforgettable	
Healed		Grateful	
Encouraged		Filled	
Known		At Home	
Forgiven		Peaceful	
Refreshed		Selfless	
On Purpose		Perseverance	

On a good day, enjoy yourself;
On a bad day, examine your conscience.
God arranges for both kinds of days
So that we won't take anything for granted.
—Ecclesiastes 7:14, MSG

Final Words

Thank you to the people who have given us our favorite names.

From Emma:

To my dad, who calls me Beautiful: Thanks for inspiring me to serve the Lord in the church. You're an amazing role model. I hope to grow to have a faith like yours. You are my rock, and I know you will never let me fall.

To my mom, who calls me SissyGirl: You have supported me in everything I do and give me endless advice that I will forever cherish. Thank you for being my BFF and binge watching countless shows with me.

To my brother, who calls me Emmy: Even though you tell me we can't be friends and siblings at the same time, I still know that you are my best friend. Thank you for putting up with me and going with me at 8pm to get McFlurries.

To Popsy who calls me Miss Emma and Mimi who calls me Sweet Emma: Thank you so much for encouraging me to sing and grow into the person I am today! I don't know what I would do without your support.

To my squad, who call me Friend: Faith, Kira, Kristen, Paloma, Danae, Charis and Zoe. You guys have always stood beside me, and I am so grateful. They say the friends you surround yourself with determine who you will grow to be. I am comforted to know that you all will help me grow stronger in my faith.

To Cho and Angela who call me Em: Both of you have helped me grow and be comfortable with who I am in Christ. I won't forget all the laughter and advice we have shared. Thank you so much for encouraging and supporting me even at my impossibly long choir concert.

From Lori:

To my husband, who calls me Babe: Jud, I have the deepest love and most profound respect for you. I am so thankful the Lord joined our lives together over twenty years ago. I wouldn't want to adventure through life with anyone else.

To Emma and Ethan, who call me Mom: I am so proud God chose me to be your mom. He beautifully created each of you on purpose, with a purpose, and for a purpose. Keep following hard after Jesus. You are world changers. I love you.

To my dad, who calls me Kiddo, and my mom, who calls me Sissy: Thank you for always believing in me, encouraging me, and making me feel like I could conquer any challenge. You have loved your children big and loved Jesus even bigger.

To my brother, who calls me Sis, and my sister-in-law, who calls me Girl: You are more than family; you are also heart-to-heart, share-anything friends. I cherish you both. More than you'll ever know.

To my tribe, who call me Friend: Brandi, Lisa H., Julie, Nicole, Laura, Nat, Whit, Linds, Lisa B., Kimberly, and Hosanna. You are my people. The ones I lean on and stand with in good times and bad. Don't know what I'd do without you.

To the Leading and Loving It team, who call me Fearless Leader: You are the dream team. Amazing sharers of wisdom and biblical insight. Your heart for other women in ministry is unmatched. It is an honor to serve alongside you. A special shout out to Linda, Liz, Cindy, Stephanie, Evelyn, Brett and Lalani for your contributions to this project.

To the Central family, who have called me Mrs. Pastor: Jud and I are so incredibly thankful God has called us to serve you. Thank you for letting us be a tiny part of Jesus changing lives here.

Notes

1. "Kintsugi/Kintsukuroi: Golden Jointery," Lakeside Pottery, www.lakesidepottery.com/Pages/kintsugi-repairing-ceramic-with-gold-and-lacquer-better-than-new.htm.

2. Seidler, Linda. Leading and Loving It Equip Team. Contributor.

3. Catfish, dir. Ariel Schulman and Henry Joost (Universal, 2010).

4. Seidler, Linda. Leading and Loving It Equip Team. Contributor.

5. Tara Conry, "Running a Marathon: What Happens to Your Body?" Newsday, May 7, 2017, www.newsday.com/news/health/running-a-marathon-what-happens-to-your-body-1.11717907.

6. Sarno, Liz. Leading and Loving It Connect Team. Contributor.

7. Seidler, Linda. Leading and Loving It Equip Team. Contributor.

8. Seidler, Linda. Leading and Loving It Equip Team. Contributor.

9. Sarno, Liz. Leading and Loving It Connect Team. Contributor.

10. Sarno, Liz. Leading and Loving It Connect Team. Contributor.

11. Beall, Cindy. Leading and Loving It Equip Team. Contributor.

12. Cited in Linda Dillow, Calm My Anxious Heart: A Woman's Guide to Finding Contentment (Colorado Springs: NavPress, 2010), 79.

13. Associated Press, "Man Survives 60 Hours at Bottom of Atlantic,

Rescued After Finding Air Pocket in Tugboat," Fox News World, December 4 2013, www.foxnews.com/world/2013/12/04/man-survives-60-hours-at-bottom-atlantic-rescued-after-finding-air-pocket-in.html.

14. Sarno, Liz. Leading and Loving It Connect Team. Contributor.

15. Sarno, Liz. Leading and Loving It Connect Team. Contributor.

16. Shouse, Stephanie. Leading and Loving It Connect Team. Contributor.

17. Daniel P. Finney, "They Met As Enemies in World War II and Became Friends 50 Years Later," USA Today News, June 6, 2017, www.usatoday.com/story/news/nation-now/2017/06/06/they-met-enemies-world-war-ii-and-became-friends-50-years-later/372969001/.

18. Cindy Boren, "Pro Surfer Mick Fanning Fights Off Terrifying Shark Attack," Washington Post, July 20, 2015, www.washingtonpost.com/news/early-lead/wp/2015/07/19/pro-surfer-fights-off-shark-attack-during-competition-in-south-africa/.

19. "Nevertheless, She Persisted," episode 22 of season 2, Supergirl, CBS, originally aired May 22, 2017.

20. Dr. Seuss, The Cat in the Hat (Boston: Houghton Mifflin, 1957), 18.

23. Detken, Brett. Leading and Loving It Equip Team. Contributor.

24. Jess, "Not a Perfect Mom, but an Enough Mom," Wonderoak, March 27, 2017, wonderoak.com/2017/03/27/not-a-perfect-mom-but-an-enough-mom/.

Lori Wilhite is the founder of Leading and Loving It - a ministry dedicated to equipping, connecting and impacting pastors' wives and women in leadership. She hopes to encourage healthy women therefore building healthy marriages, healthy families, and healthy ministries. Her first book, co-authored with Brandi Wilson, is Leading and Loving It: Encouragement for Pastors' Wives and Women in Leadership.

Lori serves alongside her husband, Jud Wilhite, at Central Church in Las Vegas. Together they love watching God change Sin City into Grace City. They have two hilarious and amazing kids, Emma and Ethan, and one stinky bulldog.

Emma Wilhite is a Senior in high school and enjoys singing in the school choir and performance groups. She loves being part of the weekend worship team and youth worship team at Central Church in Las Vegas. She is mostly made up of no sleep and procrastination.

Stay connected with

Leading
and
loving
it

online or on the app.

leadingandlovingit.com